Business Communication

(A Simplified Approach)

Sangeeta Magan

Published by:
biztantra
Management for the Flat World!
An Imprint of dreamtech PRESS

ISBN: 978-81-7722-828-1

Edition: 2018

Printed at: Reva Printers, Delhi

Dedicated

To

Punam and Baldev Gadhok

Mom and Dad, I love you.

Always did and always will!

FOREWORD

'Then you should say what you mean,' the March Hare went on. 'I do,' Alice hastily replied; 'at least I mean what I say — that's the same thing you know.' 'Not the same thing a bit!' said the Hatter. 'Why, you might just as well say that "I see what I eat" is the same thing as "I eat what I see!"'

(Lewis Carroll, Alice in Wonderland)

Communicating effectively should be the simplest thing in the world, shouldn't it? We communicate all day, i.e., talk and listen – don't we? **OR** do we?

But then is that all there is to it? Whenever things go wrong in an organization or a personal relationship, communication or rather lack of it or misinterpreting it, is often at the heart of the problem.

Improving your communication skills can bring huge rewards; it can help you to win more contracts and sales, gain promotion, manage your organization or your team more effectively. Good communication Skills can enhance relationships both at work and at home. So it's worth getting it right isn't it?

It is my pleasure to write this foreword to Prof. Sangeeta Magan's book on Business Communication, as it provides tips and techniques to enhance communication skills. It has been written in a clear and lucid language and is a must for all budding Managers and for all those who wish to survive today's cut-throat competition in the business world.

The book will help you to achieve verbal, vocal and visual success in your professional as well as personal life.

I congratulate Prof. **Sangeeta Magan** and wish her success.

Prof. (Dr) Deepak Bharioke

HOD New Delhi Institute of Management

Former Director New Delhi Institute of Management

Ex Head- Competency Development Centre, Perot Systems Ltd.

Ex Head- Instructional Resource Centre, YMCA Institute of Engineering, Faridabad.

Ex Director IIHT

Preface

Fair or not, we need to understand that the ability to communicate correctly and effectively is the skill on which a good portion of our success depends. Communication skills are prerequisite to personal, academic and professional success.

The bottom line of any profession is to earn; to earn not only profit but to earn goodwill as well. And that's what makes Business Communication an important subject to be studied by every budding manager.

It is a matter of great pleasure to bring out the first edition of my book on Business Communication. This book deals with all aspects of communication required for today's Business world.

This book has been divided into three Sections: the first deals with the basics of communication, the second with the basics of correspondence and the third with the basics of grammar.

The section 'The Basics of Communication' deals with the importance of communication and ways and means to make all types of communication more effective.

It deals with verbal as well as with non verbal means of communication, the various barriers and ways to overcome the same to make communication more effective.

'The Basics of Correspondence' deals with the written communication in the business world. Business Communication is an art and a budding manager should excel at it.

The last part of the book deals with the basics of grammar. Although some topics have been dealt with in depth but this has been done not to make you a Grammarian but to help you refine your communication and also to help you avoid common errors in your written as well as oral communication.

People associate grammar with errors and correctness. But knowing about grammar also helps us understand what makes sentences and paragraphs clear and interesting and precise.

Effectively communicating ideas, information and emotions is fundamental to our personal and professional lives. Good communication skills are rooted in:

- grammatical rules – the relationships among the working parts of language
- good mechanics to provide acceptable style
- using generally accepted words and expressions

It is in practicing grammar that we learn the crafting of clear, effective sentences.

With a foundation in grammar, we can move on to speak effectively and understand others, organize thoughts logically and express ourselves through the written word.

As a budding manager, you need to keep in mind that this is probably the last opportunity to learn the language skills before you step out into the business world.

And always remember, 'For a good tomorrow, you need to better your today!'

So go ahead, arm yourself with excellent communication skills and wish you all the best for your career!

God bless you!

- Sangeeta Magan

Acknowledgement

This is a great opportunity to express my respect to and regard for my parents for all they have done and continue to do for me. The unconditional support and encouragement has made it possible for me to be what I am today.

They were and are always there to listen and to give advice.

I deeply acknowledge the support and inspiration given by my family- my husband and my children, without which this book would not have been possible.

They have given me a quiet space to write, cooked my meals while I was working, brought me tea when I needed a break, and even read over the book for me to make sure it was likeable and useful and not just another book on Business communication.

I also acknowledge the encouragement given by my friends and all my well wishers.

Last but not the least, I acknowledge the Biztantra team for their interest in my work.

Thank you all!

- Sangeeta Magan

PART 1

THE BASICS OF COMMUNICATION

PART 2

THE BASICS OF CORRESPONDENCE

PART 3

THE BASICS OF GRAMMAR

PART 1

THE BASICS OF COMMUNICATION

Chapter 1

Communication

Learning Objectives

- To understand the Meaning of Communication
- To know the Importance of Communication
- To study the Objectives of Communication
- To know the Process of Communication

Meaning

Communication, basically, means to convey facts, ideas, feelings and thoughts. It is in fact the most important activity for social living. Communication may be verbal or nonverbal but the basic objective remains the same. Therefore in an organization, the importance of communication cannot be denied. Whether it is between the management and the employees or among the employees or even between the organization and its customer, communication needs to be very effective for the success, the organization wishes to attain.

Thus it is very important for all to have good or rather excellent communication skills. When we talk of business communication, we need to understand that effective communication ushers progress and on the other hand ineffective communication leads to misunderstandings and ultimately to downfall. Therefore for a manager, to manage an organization, it is very important to have a very good command over communication skills.

The bottom line is to earn, to earn profit as well as to earn goodwill. And that's what makes Business Communication an important subject to be studied by every budding manager.

Business Communication talks about how to relay information within and liaise with others in the supply chain, how best to promote a product or a service. And is very intricately linked to Marketing, Branding, Consumer & Public Relations, Advertising, Human resource Management etc, i.e. all Managerial activities. Business Communication is an art and to excel at it we need to understand Verbal and Non-verbal forms of communication.

Importance of Business Communication

Business communication is the most important ingredient of any business. However small or big a business may be, its success depends on how effective its communication system is, whether it is within the organization or outside organization. Inaccurate or ineffective communication may lead to conflicts within the organization and loss of goodwill outside it. Communication skills are prerequisite to personal, academic and professional success.

- Good communications skills help young managers to kick start their career, In fact, according to a study the basic skills required at the entry level of today's jobs are communication skills, and this includes all aspects of communication that is, oral , written and the listening skills.
- Even for building good relations in any profession, you require good interpersonal skills for which in turn you require excellent communication skills.
- For every profession, communiction skills are important, as they help in smooth and effective working of an organization.
- Good communication skills can enhance your career growth, personality and you have the confidence to influence and to motivate rather than just command and control.
- Effective Communication can help in achieving organizational success as well because the satisfaction level of the employees increases and hence the productivity level multiplies.
- Even an individual's own effectiveness increases by enhancing communication skills.

Thus as it is in the interest of both an individual and an organization, it becomes very important for all to study Business Communication and understand and adopt the various techniques that can help to enhance the productivity of all, thereby looking forward to success.

Objectives

To exchange information

The most important and the basic purpose of communication is exchange of information. In an organization, the management needs to keep its employees well informed about their role and responsibility in the organization and about the goals, policies and rules of the organization. Well informed employees always perform better and the environment is also more conducive, hence the productivity is more. The organizational goals can be achieved.

Similarly, if an organization communicates effectively with its clients, the clients are more satisfied and the organization improves its image in the market.

There are various ways of communicating both inside and outside the company. Inside, the company communicates with its employees through various channels of communication and the information flows in various directions as well. The communication may be either written, in the form of e-mails, notices, messages, memos, etc., OR oral, over the telephone, meetings, face-to-face, etc.

Outside the company, the advertisements, fliers, trade fairs, letters to existing and prospective clients, etc help to communicate with the world.

To provide advice and counseling

It is the duty of the managers or superiors to provide assistance to their subordinates in the task assigned to them. The advice and counseling may be either on official or on personal matters. This becomes important so as to improve the productivity of the subordinates and hence the organization.

The official advice may be related to a particular task or the goals, policies and rules of the organization.

The manager also needs to take care that his team members are not under undue stress. Psychological counseling can help to de-stress a person and improve his performance.

To issue orders and instructions

Another purpose of communication is to issue orders and give instructions to the employees as to how a task needs to be done. The orders and instructions are based on the authority of the superior and the subordinates are expected to follow them. These again maybe given in a written form or orally as the need may be. But the important fact to remember here is that the orders and the instructions always travel Downwards in the hierarchical pyramid, or are one-way flow only.

An important thing to remember is that the orders and instructions should be properly communicated in a clear language to avoid any miscommunication. It becomes the duty of the manager to ascertain that the message is received well in time and understood by the receivers.

To impart education and training

To ensure that the employees continue to update themselves, it is important for the management to provide training sessions for them. These days MDPs [Management Development Programmes] are very frequently organized by the organizations. The organizations incur large amounts of expenditure on training programmes.

Communication is also used for the purpose of educating the masses about the products and services of the organization. Unless the consumers are made aware of the products and services, they will not use them. The price, the quality, the uses, the USP, etc are some of the important factors that every consumer needs to be made aware of, and this is done through advertisements in the newspaper, magazines, etc.

To motivate

Motivation energizes and activates a person and channelizes his entire energy and attitude towards the attainment of the desired goals and hence the organizational success. A good manager should know how to motivate his / her team, so that he need not order them to work. Motivated people work harder and perform better.

To motivate subordinate, a manager needs good communication skills or rather people's skills as we call them. An organization can motivate its employees by providing them incentives. Monetary benefits are perhaps the most effective form of motivation. Other ways can be in the form of appreciation awards, even simple praise for outstanding efforts sometimes can increase the productivity of employees.

To raise morale

High morale and efficient performance go hand in hand. An efficient system of communication helps to boost the morale of the employees. If there is a positive and conducive environment in the organization, the morale of the employees is high. The high morale leads the organization to its desired goals. Care needs to be taken that the policies of the organization do not reflect any negative attitude towards the employees. The direction of communication also matters as only downward communication does not help in raising the morale of the subordinates, even the upward communication needs to be promoted. Upward communication helps to release pent-up emotions and de-stress the employees. And in today's scenario this is very much required. A healthy environment, minus negative approach and minus rumours helps an organization to move ahead towards its desired goals.

To give suggestion

Good ideas on a subject may come from all working in an organization. It is usually observed that suggestion boxes are maintained in the organizations, these days. This is actually improving the upward communication and letting the employees know that their opinion also matters. Obviously, this leads to motivated and happy employees and hence the organization grows.

To persuade

Persuasion means, 'to influence the beliefs and attitude of others'. The success of any business depends on the art of selling of its services or products. And persuasion is an art which everyone needs to excel. Good communication skills, both oral and written, are helpful in developing good persuasion skills.

To warn

Although harsh, but warning is an objective of communication. It may involve warning subordinates on account of their misbehavior, negligence, defiance of rules, and lack of punctuality or any other action on the part of the employee which could harm the organization or its image in the business world.

The Process of Communication

Communication is a process that involves at least two people; Sender and Receiver. And the purpose of communication is achieved only when the receiver decodes the message and understands it the way the sender wanted him to.

The process of communication includes the following elements:

Fig. 1.1 The Process of Communication

The Sender

The process begins with the sender who sends across the message.

The Message

The message could be written, oral or even nonverbal.

Encoding

The sender decides the most appropriate words [if the communication is to be verbal] or nonverbal methods to send the message. This process is called encoding. The sender organizes his ideas properly so that the message he wishes to send is received by the receiver as he intends.

The Channel

The sender has to decide on the channel through which he intends to convey the message. Whether the channel is to be a formal or informal depends on who is the receiver. Therefore the choice of a proper channel is an important one, so as to make the communication process most effective.

The Receiver

Obviously the purpose of communication fails if there is no receiver. The receiver has to receive the message and take further action.

Decoding

The receiver then translates the message to understand it and decoding does just this.

Feedback

The message sent by the sender, may require the receiver to send across an answer or feedback. The communication therefore becomes a circular process. The feedback is also important so as to know the response of the receiver about the message. Whether he has understood it completely or requires some clarification, whether or not he is happy to receive the message is all clear only after the feedback. Feedback may also be either verbal or nonverbal as the situation requires.

Test Yourself

1. What is Communication?
2. Discuss the importance of Communication.
3. What are the objectives of Communication?
4. Explain the process of Communication.
5. Write a short note on the elements of the communication process.

Chapter 2

Means of Business Communication

Learning Objectives

- To get introduced to various Means of Communication
- To understand Verbal Communication & its Types
- To understand Oral Communication
- To study the Advantages of Oral Communication
- To study the Limitations of Oral Communication
- To know about Written Communication
- To study the Advantages of Written Communication
- To study the Limitations of Written Communication

Introduction to Various Means/Media of Communication

Communication is possible through various means or media as we call them. The choice of the media depends on the purpose of the information that needs to be sent across.

For example, if the information is to be sent across to the general public, we may use print media or the radio or the television. We use notices for information to be given to students in a school or college or to people working in an organization. Emails, sms, etc are getting popular to send messages, thereby saving paper.

And of course there are the Oral means and the Non verbal means of communication as well. It may sound strange but a lot can be conveyed even without uttering a single word. Our actions, body language, paralanguage and even silence are yet other means of communication.

Media/Means of Communication

Fig. 2.1 Media/Means of Communication

Verbal

- Oral
- Written

Nonverbal

- Appearance
- Sign language
- Body language
- Paralanguage
- Timing
- Space
- Silence
- Listening

Verbal Communication

Verbal communication, basically, means putting into words, or in other words, using a language to convey a message. The two means of Verbal communication are the oral media and the written media.

Both are equally important and powerful means of communication and again the choice of the media depends on our requirement. Advantages and limitations are there in both cases as we will study further in this chapter. But the most important thing that we must keep in mind here is that the language that we use, for either the Oral or the Written must be grammatically correct.

In today's globalized scenario, the usage of English language has had an exponential growth. It has become the global language for business and international relations. Although, it is not an official language of many countries but it is taught as the second language.

Business communication, therefore, has become important for all those eyeing the global competitive business, as it enhances the chances of doing business with companies from English speaking nations.

To cut across the language barrier and to have an edge, it is necessary to be fluent in Oral and Written skills of the language. Although sad, but it is observed that sometimes people fail in their quest of business or professional success because of the basic reason of language becoming a barrier.

The choice of the means of communication depends on our requirement. It can depend on factors like the speed or urgency of the message, the secrecy and the legal validity required, etc.

Oral Communication

A child learns to speak much before he learns to write. It is the most widely used means of communication and plays a very important role in maintaining good relations whether it is between two persons or amongst many people. Oral communication has its importance in families, between friends, in organizations and almost everywhere.

Ineffective oral communication or miscommunication can hamper relations and hinder and growth. Oral communication can take the form of speeches, discussions, debates, face to face talk and telephonic conversations and can be either formal or informal.

One important principle to be followed or remembered is the 'KISS Principle- 'keep it short and simple'.

This is to make the oral communication more effective and easier for the receiver to understand and convey it further down the line as and when required.

Advantages of Oral Communication

'Saves paper'

In today's scenario saving on paper has become an important issue. And oral communication can definitely help us to do the same.

'Saves time'

Considerable amount of precious time is lost in writing out a message and then sending it to the receiver to read. Oral communication can help us to save our precious time.

'Saves money'

Time saved is money saved for an organization, which can be used for more constructive and productive work. Also the money spent on stationery can be cut down considerably.

'More powerful'

Oral messages are much more powerful as they can help people to be more persuasive.

'Builds better relations'

When we communicate orally, we can build and maintain better relations with our colleagues and others working in the organization and with our customers and suppliers. Oral communication adds a personal touch to and therefore develops better interpersonal relationships.

'Conveys clearer meaning'

Our voice modulation, i.e. the tone, pitch and loudness of the voice can help to convey messages more clearly.

'Immediate feedback'

When communication is oral, immediate response and reaction with can be clarified which cuts down on miscommunication in the organization. This in turn helps the organization to reach a conclusion faster and more efficiently.

Limitations of Oral Communication

'Not for lengthy messages'

Too lengthy messages may turn out to be boring and thereby the listeners may lose interest and may in turn miss out on vital points. Also remembering all that was said is difficult for the speaker as well as for the listeners.

'No legal validity'

Unless and until a spoken message is recorded, it can have no legal validity.

'May create misunderstanding'

An oral message can lead to misunderstanding if the speaker has not organized his thoughts and words carefully. Although oral communication can have room for clarifications later on but a lot of precious time is lost in the process. Sometimes this can lead to disastrous effects in the business. Words once uttered cannot be erased. Therefore we need to be very careful in our choice of words.

'Constrained by various barriers'

Since the process of communication is not complete by speaking alone, the understanding of the message is equally important for the same. And understanding an oral message is definitely constrained by a lot many barriers like noise, language, accent, etc [later discussed in chapter 6].

Written Communication

Although oral communication comes spontaneously to man, and written communication requires a lot many years of hard work, however words once said may be forgotten but written words become permanent.

Also whereas oral communication is an important means in a business or an organization, we cannot take written communication to be an unimportant means as well. It is as indispensable as oral means.

Written communication can be in the form of notices, messages, circulars, reports, emails, etc. The characteristics and the layout of each have been discussed in the later part of the book.

It is very important to understand that writing is an art and it requires a lot of effort. Creativity and excellence in the language used are essentially required for the written communication to be good.

Advantages of Written Communication

'On Records'

Everything can be on records from correspondence with clients and dealers, minutes of important meetings, etc.

Just imagine getting an oral appointment letter, would you not worry about the profile and the benefits, since nothing is on record, things could change as per the employers.

Therefore written documents provide a permanent record and are beneficial for future references as well as for formulating policies and deciding targets for the future.

'Legal Validity'

Written records have legal validity and may be used for building up legal defenses in an organization.

'Fast and Inexpensive'

Emails are in fact the most inexpensive and fastest means of communication when face to face communication is not possible.

'Accurate and Dependable'

Written words are definitely considered to be accurate and more dependable than oral words, because oral words may later be changed whereas written messages are permanent. Nobody can go back on their words, provided the words are written.

'Well formulated'

Spoken words can be spontaneous but written words can always be given a thought, drafted and conveyed carefully in a well formulated manner. Hence this message is clearer and more specific.

'Assigns Responsibility'

Everyone in an organization cannot be told to do everything. For every smallest task to be done, responsibility needs to be assigned. And for this written communication is obviously the most effective means. Orally conveyed responsibilities may never be taken seriously.

'Lesser Chances of Misunderstanding'

If the language is grammatically correct, then there are lesser chances of any misunderstanding. Of course incorrect usage of grammar can lead to a bigger misunderstanding.

'Pen is mightier than the sword'

We all know this proverb and understand its meaning. Written word carries more weight and is therefore more authoritative and formal than oral word.

'Permit Revision'

Written words can be erased or revised as per our requirement, of course before sending the message through.

Limitations of Written Communication

'Time Consuming'

Written communication requires a lot of time to put into words, one's thoughts and formulation of the same is of course time consuming, as proper structuring is required.

'Money Consuming'

A large amount of the resources are wasted in an organization on stationary and storage of files and records. Of course computers have helped us to save or rather just cut down on some of these expenses but yet it costs a lot to an organization and of course the environment as well because paper means cutting of trees.

'Requires Literate skill'

Proper grammatical knowledge of a language is required to communicate effectively. And written communication is constrained by grammar and of course the handwriting if the records are not typed.

Also if poorly drafted messages are sent, it can cost an organization, its business as well.

Test Yourself

1. Compare and contrast the advantages of Oral & Written communication.
2. Compare and contrast the limitations of Oral & Written Communication.
3. A good system of communication makes use of both oral as well as written means of communication'. Comment.
4. 'Both oral as well as written means are indispensable'. Explain with examples.

Chapter 3

Listening Skills

Learning Objectives

- To study the Importance of Listening
- To know the Types of Listening
- To understand the Barriers to Effective Listening
- To know how to make Listening Effective
- To study the 10 Commandments of Listening

'Don't just hear, listen!'

Importance of Listening

What good would an oral message do, if there were no one to listen? Often when there is a conflict or a misunderstanding, the reason is communication gap. That means the communication process is not complete if there is either no speaker or no listener.

Although listening is not an important part of the communication process, it is actually sad that people listen less and speak more.

But we now realize the importance of listening in all Business situations.

To maintain good relations with all inside an organization and our clients and dealers, it is very important for us to learn to be good listeners.

'A good listener is always a good speaker.' This proverb holds good because we need to understand that when we listen, we gather information, and only a well informed person can himself be a good speaker. Poor listening skills can lead to many problems not only in our professional life but also in our personal life. Many a times, we hear youngsters talking about 'Generation Gap' between themselves and their elders, but frankly it is only communication gap that causes any conflict.

We all need to listen empathically to build healthy human relations in our personal as well as in our professional life.

As a manager as well one needs to enhance his/her listening skills as one needs to listen as much as talk in this profession. No sales person can ever satisfy a customer unless and until he or she listens to the customer's requirement or even a complaint.

Listening also has a positive influence. It may be surprising but by listening effectively to people, we help them to gain confidence, thereby increasing their productivity as well.

A manager can gain trust, respect and loyalty of the team if he is a good listener.

Types of Listening

Passive Listening

In this case, the listener is just probably pretending to listen and is otherwise indifferent to what is being said.

Here we can say that only hearing is taking place. The barriers may be many and are discussed later in this chapter. But the important thing to understand is that since listening is passive, the message is not listened to properly, and thereby cannot be ever recalled at any point in the future.

The listener may nod and smile at all right places but actually does not listen anything that is said, because, often the listening process stops at hearing and there is no effort to further process or comprehend the message.

'Selective Listening'

When listening is done according to one's whims and wishes, the listener selects the part that he is desirous of listening and ignores the rest. Selective listening takes place when the listener is not focused and his mind keeps wandering.

The reasons can be many – may be the listener is not in a condition to focus or concentrate as his mind is on other issues or elsewhere. Sometimes selective listening can be embarrassing if a sudden opinion is asked, and the listener has been tuning in and out.

The reasons may be many, the listener may not be in a position to concentrate, or may consider the speaker to be poorly informed on the subject.

'Emphatic Listening'

Listening that involves eyes and heart along with ears is emphatic listening. The listening is done so intensively that the speaker is well understood, both intellectually and emotionally. But there is a risk here as well; the listener is vulnerable to the speaker's influence.

'Active Listening'

The most desirable of all types is active listening, or attentive listening. Here the listener is actively and attentively concentrating on the words being spoken.

This demonstrates the interest of the listener and thereby motivates and encourages the speaker to continue speaking. This also shows regard for the speaker and the listener is in a better position to comprehend a message, to remember and recall the same in the future.

This type of listening not only helps the listener to decode the message properly, but also makes it easy for the speaker to deliver the message in a meaningful manner.

Barriers To Effective Listening

Broadly the 'Barriers' can be classified or grouped under three main categories:

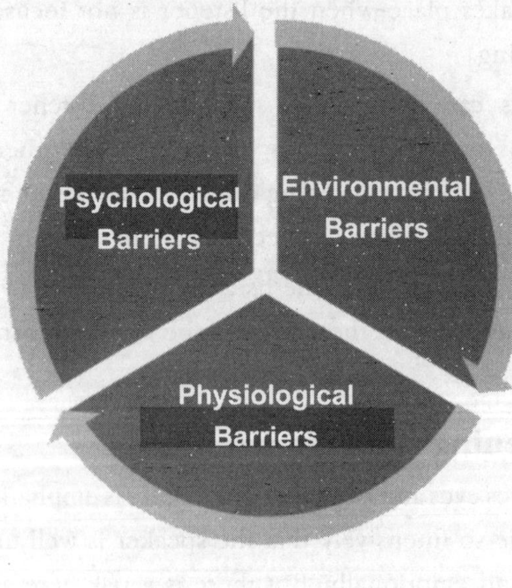

Fig. 3.1
Barriers to Effective Listening

'Environmental Barriers'

The environmental or physical barriers include the acoustics and related factors like the malfunctioning of the sound system or the transmission failure.

Sometimes the speaker is too close or too far from the microphone which is also an important barrier. In fact, while speaking, the speaker, sometimes turns his head to look at the screen behind him while giving a presentation, thereby half the sentence does not reach the microphone or the audience properly.

Noise is another important physical barrier to listening. Any kind of noise, whether the sound of an air conditioner or a ringing phone etc. distracts a listener and thereby he loses his concentration and, as a result, is unable to receive the message effectively.

'Physiological Barriers'

Such barriers arise when the listener is not physiologically active. This may be due to many factors. The listener may be in ill health or just tired or sleepy. Even if the listener is not sitting comfortably, he or she is unable to concentrate on the words of the speaker. Sometimes the listener is so engrossed in his own worries or work that he may find it hard to concentrate and listen effectively. Physiological barriers may also be because of the accent and pronunciation short comings of the speaker.

'Psychological Barriers'

Barriers like prejudice, apathy or fear are common psychological barriers. These include values and behavioral aspects like beliefs, bias, likes and dislikes, attitudes, etc. Sometimes it is past experiences, discomfort with the topic of the talk or lack of credibility of the speaker that acts as a psychological barrier. The listener may have a self-centered attitude or in other words may be an egoist. Listening requires an open mind and a heart that are free from any kind of negative feelings, because if our heart and mind are not open, we cannot receive the message and comprehend it effectively.

How to make Listening Effective?

To improve your listening skills the most important thing is, 'you must want to improve'. We must remember that we get more influenced by what we hear than by what we read. The way small kids remember stories told by grandmothers is amazing. They recall them even after years of hearing them.

Of course, now as grown ups we find it hard to pay attention, because we may consider it to be 'work' and that is something we may want to avoid doing.

The actual use of communication skills should be as follows:

Writing	9%
Reading	16%
Speaking	30%
Listening	45%

But ironically it is not so. It is in fact as follows:

Reading	52%
Writing	30%
Speaking	10%
Listening	8%

And when in today's business scenario, where no business can thrive without effective communication, can we afford to overlook this aspect?

There are some well accepted commandments of listening, following which it may be possible to remove the barriers that come in the way of effective listening and hinder the communication process.

10 Commandments of Listening

'Stop talking'

God has given us two ears and one mouth, so why not use them in that order. So talk less and listen more.

It so happens that even if we are listening, we are thinking about what to say next rather than listening to the speaker. So the first rule says to stop talking and start listening.

'Put the speaker at ease'

When we listen actively we help to put the speaker at ease and he is able to deliver more effectively and meaningfully.

And if the message gets across effectively, we have better inputs to work with.

'Show that you want to listen'

If the listener is able to convince the speaker that he is attentively listening to what he is speaking, he performs better. Nobody wishes to talk to a bored audience.

'Remove distractions'

Any distractions, such as ringing mobiles, continuous shuffling of papers, outside noise, etc. can hinder the listening process. Therefore it is very important to review these.

'Empathize with the speaker'

We need to put ourselves in the speaker's shoes to understand his feelings of talking to a disinterested audience.

The speaker may not be perfect, but for a true exchange of information it is necessary to overlook any shortcomings and create an environment of understanding.

'Be patient'

Every person has his own way of delivering a talk. We need to give him enough time to complete what he wants to say rather than interrupt and disturb his train of thought. So a listener needs to be both attentive as well as patient

'Hold your temper'

Temper impedes the communication and angry people never listen to each other. They just speak to each other and get more and more angry. It so happens, that anger blocks minds to the words of others.

'Avoid arguments and criticisms'

Rarely does anyone benefit from argument and criticism. When we criticize or argue with a person, he too, either gets angry and the conflict goes on or he would clam up and refrain from further talk. So either way, neither of them benefits.

'Ask questions'

When we ask questions, we display our interest in the talk and regard for the speaker. This of course, not only helps the listener to listen effectively but also the speaker to deliver his message effectively.

'Stop talking'

The first commandment was, 'stop talking' as we need to first stop talking, to listen to a speaker and the last commandment again is the same as all the other commandments depend on it.

Test Yourself

1. 'A Good speaker is always a Good listener'. Comment.
2. Explain the different types of listening.
3. What are the barriers to good listening skills?
4. How can you make your listening effective?
5. What are the 10 commandments of good listening?

Chapter 4

Means of Non-Verbal Communication

Learning Objectives

- To know the Importance of Non-verbal Communication
- To study about Body Language
- To understand Paralanguage

Importance of Non-Verbal Communication

Till now, we have been talking about speaking and listening skills, but yet, there is another important aspect of communication and that is, Non-verbal communication.

Communication without words, strange as it may sound, is a very important aspect even of Business Communication.

Even without utterance of a single word, we convey a lot by our gestures, touch, body language, posture, facial expressions and eye contact.

In fact, even our speech contains elements of Non-verbal communication such as Paralanguage which includes voice quality, emotion, intonation and stress.

Very rightly it is said, 'Actions speak louder than words'.

The non-verbal cues communicate our feelings during our communication with others and includes all intentional and unintentional messages.

Our smile or frown, our vibrant and confident voice, our handshake – firm or limp, all tell something to the listeners.

In fact, during the last one decade there has been a tremendous upsurge both in interest and research in the non-verbal aspects of communication. Even in a Business scenario, the knowledge and skill of non-verbal aspects can prove to be helpful.

The way one listens, looks, moves and reacts tells the other person whether he cares or not, and also how well he is listening. Non-verbal signals one sends can either produce a sense of trust and interest or can generate distrust and disinterest.

In forming and maintaining business relationships it, therefore, becomes necessary to send positives cues to show that we understand and care and of course, notice as well the efforts of others.

Both connection and trust are lost if negative non-verbal cues are sent across. And this hinders and hampers the success of any organization.

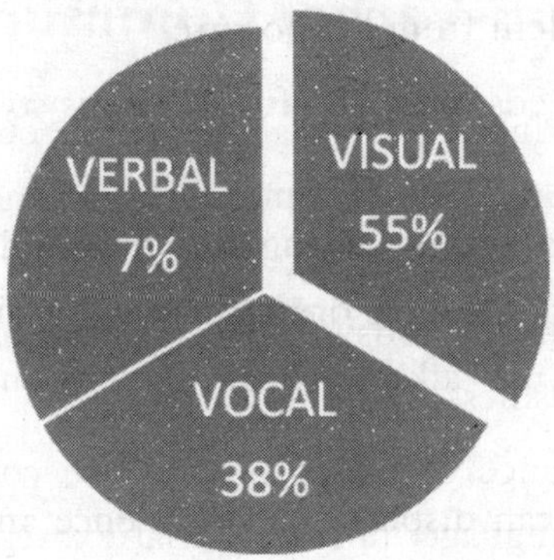

Fig. 4.1
Rule

7% 38% 55% Rule

It is actually surprising and interesting to note that 'Verbal Communication accounts for the lowest percentage according to the study by Albert Mehrabian.

From this it is very clear that we communicate not by words alone.

When we speak our 'Personality' Speaks and Personality includes the Visual, the Vocal and the Verbal aspects, all at one go.

Body Language

An important aspect of non-verbal communication is Body Language, which includes posture, gestures, facial expressions and eye movements.

'What you say' is important but 'how you say' is more important. 'Kinesics' is the study of body language.

Very rightly someone has said 'Bodies do not lie' and also 'Face is the index of the mind'. Much of the time this aspect of communication is Involuntary or Unintentional.

Gestures are the physical movements of our arms, legs hands, head, in fact all our body parts. The movements or gestures compliment and reinforce our speech.

The way a person stands or sits or his posture as well, all are a very important factor in non-verbal communication.

Whether a person or listener is interested in your talk, or has a laidback attitude is very evident from his posture.

Even the speaker needs to be careful about his style of standing and sitting.

The nodding of head, smiling, shrugging of shoulders, frowning, etc. are gestures that may send positive or negative vibes to the others. It is said that we need to 'walk the talk'. We need to work on this aspect of communication to be able to be successful.

Our body language can display our confidence and sincerity or give away the lack of the same.

Kinesics also includes our facial expressions.

Imagine a smile on the face of your boss or a client. Next imagine a frown on their face. How would you feel in both the circumstances?

Whether you are relaxed or tense is very much evident from your facial expressions. There is another important element of body language – Handshake.

A firm handshake or a limp handshake gives away a lot about a person. It can talk a lot without words.

Even the attire of a person can add meaning to the process of communication. As we know, 'The first impression is the last impression'.

So in order to compliment our speech we need to be sure to dress up according to the need of the hour, as appearance says it all.

The attire includes the clothing as well as accessories. The way you dress can effect or influence how people react to you.

You cannot change your physical characteristics, at least not without plastic surgery but you can enhance your looks, definitely, by your style of dressing.

BUT it is not only about 'what you wear, it is also about how you wear'.

A person who is appropriately dressed for the occasion will obviously cast a better impression on the others. Imagine a speaker on the stage or in a boardroom giving a presentation in a blue faded jeans!!!

'Apparel oft proclaims the man' said Polonius in 'Hamlet' by William Shakespeare.

Polonius advises his son,

"Costly thy habit as thy purse can buy,

but not express'd in fancy; rich, not gaudy;

for the apparel oft proclaims the man,'

In other words, we are often judged by our appearance. Our clothes should not necessarily be the most expensive, but only as expensive as we can afford, because the way we carry the attire is more important.

Paralanguage

Paralanguage means, 'like language'. And it is considered under non-verbal communication as it does not consist of words.

But again it is very closely associated with verbal communication because, although, it is not only about the words you say but it is also about 'how' you say those words.

How a speaker verbalizes his words is Paralanguage. It refers to a wide range of aspects like the tone, pitch, speed of speech, volume, usage of pauses, word stress, etc.

Good communicators or good Orators know how to use these cues effectively.

Paralanguage is a very important aspect of communication, and everyone should learn to use this element carefully and impressively.

Consider a telephonic conversation, especially the telephonic round of an interview. How does a person judge your suitability for a post by just talking to you on the phone?

Therefore we need to hone our skills of the way we say, what we say.

Let us talk of all elements of Paralanguage and understand to use them effectively.

Tone

Our voice quality has an important element – Tone. It can display appreciation or sarcasm, admiration or anger. Our tone can be gentle or aggressive.

Consider the following sentence.

'What a painting!'

Now the way the speaker says the line shows what he actually means or wishes to communicate. His tone may be full of admiration or may be full of sarcasm. Tone conveys the attitude of a person as well.

Pitch

A constant pitch creates monotony; therefore variations in pitch are an absolute necessity that is of course if we do not wish to have a bored audience listening to us. Pitch of the voice displays the mental state of person. Emotions like anger, excitement, happiness etc. all become evident. Even the confidence level of person is evident from the pitch of his voice.

Speed of Speech

You should not confuse speed with fluency, because they have a different meaning.

In fact you should not speak with a high speed always otherwise words may get mixed up, the meaning may not be clearly understood and the communication process gets hampered.

It is very necessary to maintain a balance of the speed of your speech.

Pauses

Punctuation marks like a comma and a full stop are used to show a pause in the written word, but when we deliver the words, we need to add or use pauses to be effective in our communication. Pauses at the right place can enhance our speech but too many pauses can spoil it as well.

Fillers

Words like 'um, you know, ok, right, etc, are called fillers. Judicious use is allowed but frequent use hinders and hampers the communication process.

Volume

You must have come across people talking very loudly on phone. They definitely need to understand that soft or medium volume will reach the listener as well, because the voice is not reaching directly but through the phone line.

On the other hand, consider a speaker talking to an audience without a mike. If he is not loud enough, his voice will not reach the entire audience.

So we need to learn to control our volume appropriately.

Intonation

Word stress or intonation is very crucial for effective and impressive communication. In fact by putting stress on different words, we can change the meaning of the same sentence.

Even stressing syllables in a word can enhance our pronunciation and clarity of speech.

Test Yourself

1. What is non-verbal communication?
2. What are the various aspects of body language?
3. What is Paralanguage?
4. What are the various aspects of Paralanguage?

Chapter 5

Principles of Effective Communication

Learning Objectives

- To study the Seven C's of Communication

C's of Communication

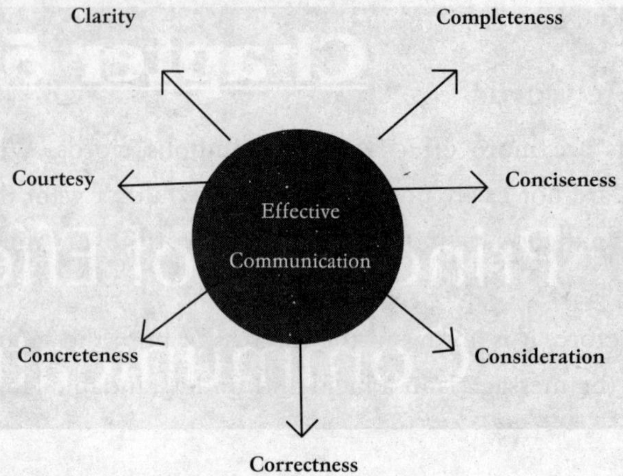

Fig. 5.1
C's of Communication

In order to make our communication, written or oral, effective, we need to keep in mind these 7 C's of communication, as they are referred to.

Let us discuss each one of them so as to be able to make our communication more effective.

Clarity

The Message that the sender wishes to send should have the same meaning for the receiver as well. For this, it is important for the sender to have both the clarity of thought as well as the clarity of expression.

The process of communication begins with the generation of an idea in the mind of the sender. But is he clear about the message, he wishes to send across?

For this a sender should be able to understand and answer the following questions:

- What is the objective of the message?
- What is the message?
- To whom do I wish to convey the message?
- Which would be the most suitable medium to convey the message most effectively?

Once the sender has clarity of thought; he needs to express the message in a clear and simple language. There is no use of sending a message if it cannot be understood correctly by the receiver.

To ensure clarity of expression the following points must be remembered always.

'Use simple words'

Simple words are more effective than pompous words. Why use the words which are not easily understood? You wouldn't want the receiver standing with a dictionary in hand to look up words every time you send him a message.

Therefore, it is always in the interest of both the sender and the receiver that the message is in a lucid and understandable language.

For example:

Avoid these	**Use these**
Facilitate	Help
Demonstrate	Show
Utilize	Use

'Try to avoid phrases'

To make our language more flowery, we tend to use more and more phrases when a single word could have been used.

For example:

Avoid these	**Use these**
'At the present moment'	now
'Despite the fact that'	although
'Will you be kind enough'	Please

'Try to use simple verbs instead of nouns'

The usage of verbs instead of nouns makes our language simpler and thus adds clarity to our words.

For example:

Avoid these	Use these
'Come to a conclusion'	Conclude
'Make the announcement'	Announce
'Take into consideration'	Consider

'Use active voice instead of passive voice'

The usage of Active voice helps to add clarity to our words whereas the passive voice is more formal and impersonal. Therefore Active voice should be preferred but sometimes we are justified in using passive voice as well, especially when a very formal and impersonal attitude is required to be shown.

Active voice also is more specific and elegant.

For example:

Passive

'It is thought that your prices are on the higher side.'

Active

'Your prices are on the higher side.'

'Avoid Jargon'

Jargon refers to the special language of a profession, trade or field although, according to the 'Thesaurus' the synonyms are disorder, jumble, chaos, confusion, etc.

Jargon has its usage in certain professions, for example legal language which is a primarily stylish and here the requirement is a formal and stiff kind of language. Even in Medical Science or any other technical field the usage of jargon is confined to words.

In a business scenario, however avoiding the usage of jargon adds more clarity and simplicity.

For example:

Avoid these

'This is to acknowledge your kind support'

Use these

'Thank you for your support'

'Avoid ambiguity'

Ambiguous sentences can have more than one meaning.

- Sometimes, the usage of personal pronouns is such that the meaning of the sentence is not clear.

For example:

Suresh told Shyam that he was not being considered for any increment. [It is not possible to understand as to who is not being considered]

- Sometimes, the punctuation marks used in a sentence make it an ambiguous sentence.

For example:

'Eats, shoots and leaves.'

The author Lynne Truss's book on grammatical errors is definitely a must read.

- Sometimes the placing of adverbs makes all the differences.

For example:

I like only you.

I only like you.

The adverb only placed at two different places in the same sentence makes all the difference.

'Avoid long sentences'

Very long unending sentences add confusion and thus the message received is not clear. So it is advisable to use short sentences to add clarity to your words.

Completeness

Communication must bc complete to avoid any confusion in the mind of the receiver. In fact if the message is incomplete, the receiver is left guessing and thus causes delay in the further action plan.

Therefore it is very important for the message to include all the required facts and details on which the further action might depend.

It is advisable to check and see whether the message answers the 'five W' questions- What, Why, When, Where, Who, before sending it across.

In a business scenario, also, the letters, notices, etc need to be complete in all aspects to make our communication effective and fast, because unclear messages delay further plans.

Conciseness

Conciseness or brevity saves time and the message is computer without being lengthy. 'Time is money', so why waste.

Say all you want to in the fewest possible words and you have saved both time and money for both yourself and the receiver.

More words never add clarity rather they tire and bore a listener or reader. Hence our message needs to be as concise as possible but of course not at the cost of other C's of communication. The message should be clear, complete, correct and courteous yet concise.

Four Simple rules may be followed to make your message a concise one.

Only relevant facts and details should be added, and all unnecessary ones should be avoided. You should avoid trite and wordy expressions to add more clarity.

For example:

'We wish to extend a warm welcome to you' can easily be substituted by 'we welcome you'.

Repetition causes monotony even if you are trying to stress a point.

And of course you need to organize your message well so as to add effectiveness to your communication.

Consideration

Never prepare a message from your point of view alone, always keep the receiver in mind as well and you can never go wrong.

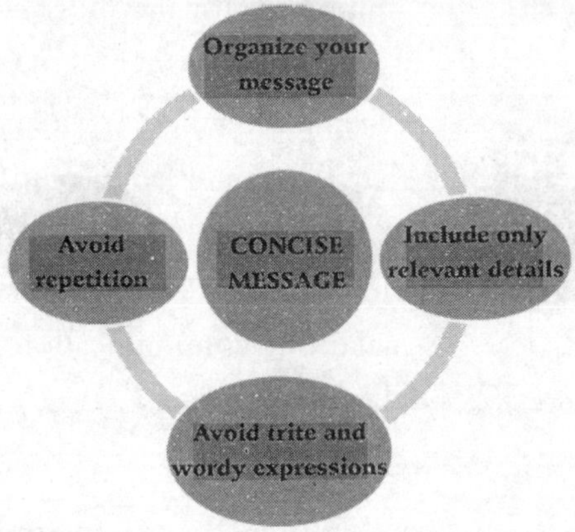

Fig. 5.2
Conciseness

The sentiments of the receiver should always be understood and kept in mind. The sender needs to adopt a more humane approach and the needs and socio-psychological background of the receiver should be understood.

'First understand then be understood' is the golden rule for communication. For this remember the following tips and you have been considerate.

Gender bias should be avoided because you need to look around and understand that the business world is no longer dominated by men. So take the following precautions:

Use words free from gender bias

For example:

- The chairperson took the right decision (Not Chairman)
- The police were handling the situation tactfully. (Not Policemen)
- The salesperson was pleasant to talk. (Not Salesman)

Use a slash to include both the alternatives

For example:

Dear Sir/Madam

Use plural forms which include both the genders

For example:

Fig. 5.3
Consideration

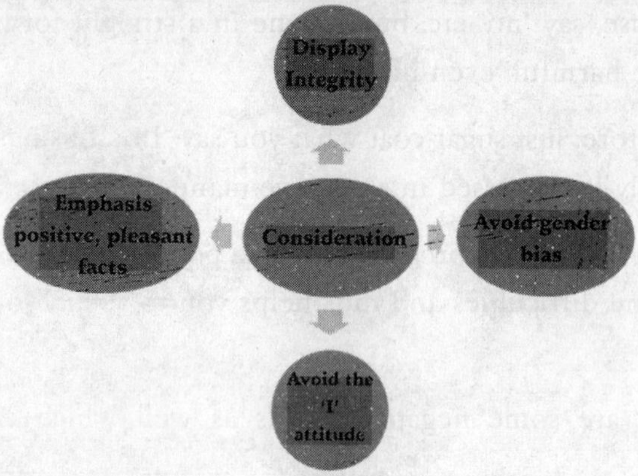

Write:

The members cast their vote.

Don't Write:

Each member cast his vote.

Use 'the' for 'his/her'

For example:

Don't write:

The manager talked to his customers.

Write:

The manager talked to the Customers.

Avoid the 'I' attitude and adopt the 'you' attitude because as discussed earlier in this chapter, all communication should keep in mind the receiver. Hence avoid using 'I' and 'We' and write 'you'.

For example:

Don't write:

'I wish to express my sincere thanks for the lovely gift I received on my birthday'.

Write:

'Thank you for the lovely gift you sent on my birthday.'

Emphasize positive, pleasant facts. Sometimes you may have to complain, refuse, say 'no' etc. but if done in a straight forward way, the impact may be harmful, even disastrous.

Therefore, just sugar-coat what you say, In a business letter all is accepted calmly if expressed in a positive manner.

In fact saying or expressing 'No' in a positive way tells the receiver of your genuine difficulties and thus helps you to retain your customers for future.

There are some negative words as well which can easily be avoided.

For example:

You walk into a showroom to buy a Television.

The salesperson leads you to the Plasma model, which you say is expensive. Then the salesperson guides to a flat screen which you probably like at first sight.

But imagine how would you feel if the salesperson were to say loudly, "This is a cheap television and this might fit your pocket?"

Instead of 'cheap' the usage of the word 'Economical' would have been more appropriate.

Integrity can never be a redundant value, even in this highly materialistic world. So go ahead and display you values.

Correctness

Correctness in Business Communication includes the format, the grammar, the punctuation and the spellings. It's always good to keep a dictionary handy, so as to look up a word rather than to make a grave mistake.

It is important for you to remember that correctness also implies giving correct facts as well.

Therefore correct facts, correct format, correct grammar, correct spellings and correct time enhance the effectiveness of the communication process.

Concreteness

Instead of vague or generalized statements, our communication needs to be specific and definite. Our words should be supported by relevant facts and figures.

Courtesy

The last but not the least is courtesy.

Courtesy and good Communication skills empower us and help us to build better relationships in, both, our personal as well as professional lives and go a long way.

In a business scenario as well this basic human value is very much required. We need to create friendliness around us whether it is between us and the others in an organization or between us and our customers and dealers.

The golden rule is 'Treat others as you wish to be treated'.

An act of courtesy will gain you many more friends than an act of rudeness or arrogance.

In the business world, we can show our courtesy in quite a few ways.

Answer letters promptly

Gone are the days when we could afford to be slow in our communication. Now in this era of cut-throat competition we need to be very prompt in answering the letter and e-mails.

Even if it is just an acknowledgement that needs to be sent across, it is considered to be an act of courtesy to be prompt.

Apologizing' for your mistake and 'thanking' generously for a favor are two important ways of showing you courtesy.

Always remember 'Courtesy begets courtesy'.

Test yourself

1. Discuss in brief the C's of Communication.
2. Write short notes on :
    a) Avoiding gender bias
    b) Courtesy in business
    c) Jargon
    d) Clarity of expression
    e) Punctuation errors

Chapter 6

Types of Communication

Learning Objectives

- To understand the Organizational Pyramid
- To study the Formal & Informal Channels of Communication
- To understand the Grapevine
- To study the Direction of Communication
- To understand Downward Communication
- To understand Upward Communication
- To study the Horizontal Communication
- To study the Diagonal Communication

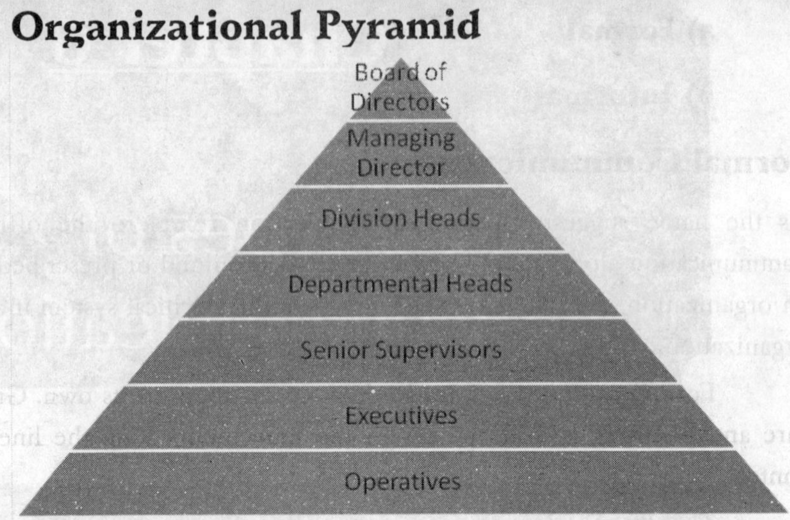

Fig. 6.1 Organizational Pyramid

Every organization has a hierarchical line of authority starting with the Board of Directors at the top to the Operative employees at the bottom. The basic structure, called the 'Organizational Pyramid' remains the same in all organizations; however the detailed structure depends on the size of the organization.

Formal & Informal Channels of Communication

In today's business environment of globalization and hence of multinational competition, communication has become an important component of all business organizations.

The size of organizations is getting bigger and bigger and hence, the need for proper and effective channels of communication has arisen.

We often hear the phrase, 'through proper channel', and to understand this phrase it is important for us to understand the Hierarchical system or the organizational pyramid talked of, earlier in this chapter.

A channel is the path along which communication may be passed on in an organization, may be either between individuals or different departments.

Channels of communication may be divided mainly into two categories:

a) Formal

b) Informal

Formal Communication

As the name suggests, formal communication refers to the official communication along a channel that is pre-determined or prescribed by an organization, and this channel follows the hierarchical system in the organization.

Formal communication just does not happen on its own. Great care and planning is done to design the movement along the line of control.

This lines of Communication usually takes the form of written Communication such as memos, letters, reports, etc. However even formal communication can be oral or even non-verbal.

Advantages of Formal Communication

This is a very systematic channel and it ensures a proper flow of information or in other words, we can say it follows the protocol.

It is considered authentic as it is a path already laid down by the organization.

This channel develops a tendency of filtering information and hence the higher level of the management doesn't get logged down with unnecessary information.

Disadvantages of Formal Communication

- It happens, that sometimes filtering the information is carried too far and the actual scene is that the flow of information is inhibited.
- The information also may get distorted according to the selfish motives of the people in the channel.
- There are always the chances of red tapism and delay tactics.
- Formal communication is time consuming and we need to remember that time means money to an organization.

- Therefore it increases the expenditure of the organization.
- Last but not the least formal communication lacks any personal touch and personal involvement. It often happens that in huge organizations, people may not even recognize each other as the communication is only formal.

Informal Communication

All communication which is not official is informal communication. 'Man is a social animal' and hence the basic instinct to communicate forgets all norms. The only norm followed is to satisfy the social needs. Informal communication may be work related or not, serious or not so serious. But usually consists of talk which mutually interests all. This kind of communication is also known as Grapevine.

The channel for Grapevine communication is not controlled by an Organization.

The Grapevine

As the origin and direction of the flow of informally conveyed information cannot be easily traced, hence the name grapevine.

Grapevine communication travels in every direction without any restrictions. Some have also named it a rumor mill. A message spreads like wildfire almost instantaneously as soon as it enters the grapevine.

The channels although unofficial, are created and controlled by the people themselves. Quite often, it also contains some useful information.

Factors Leading to the Grapevine

i. There may be a feeling of uncertainty among the employees when the organization is passing through a difficult phase.

ii. Sometimes lack of self confidence in an employee is the cause of the grapevine.

iii. Sometimes "Sycophancy" prevails in the organization and a favored group is formed, giving others a feeling of insecurity that gives way to their pent-up feelings through the grapevine.

Working of the Grapevine

The Grapevine or the informal channel of communication has been classified into four kinds of chain:-

- Single Strand chain is one in which 'A' passes a piece of information to 'B' who passes it on to 'C' and so on.
- Gossip chain is formed when a person 'A' seeks out everyone around him and passes the information to all.
- Probability chain is a random kind of a chain, where information is conveyed according to the law of probability.
- Cluster Chain is formed when a person 'A' tells a piece of information to a selective number of people, who in turn pass it on to another group of selected people.
- This selected group is one which is trusted by the 'sender'. Cluster network is the most popular channel of informal communication.

Single Strand Chain

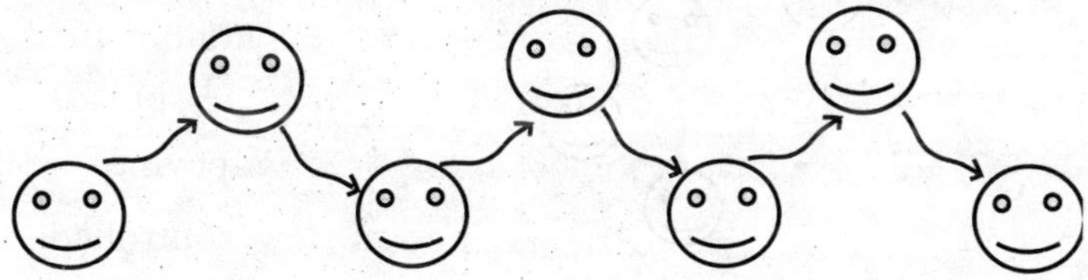

Fig. 6.2
Single Strand Chain

Gossip Chain

Fig. 6.3
Gossip Chain

Cluster Chain

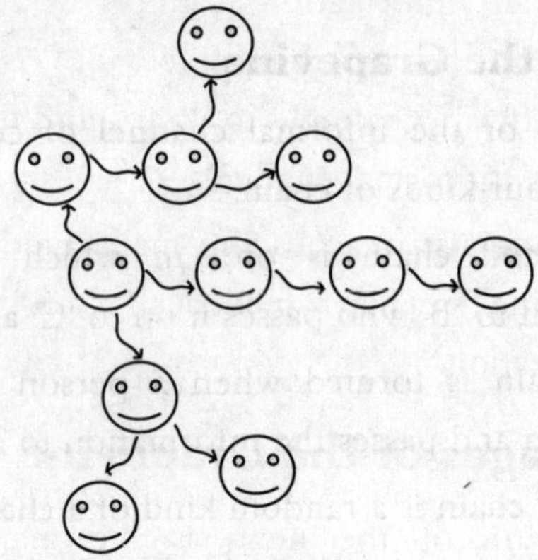

Fig. 6.3
Cluster Chain

Probability Chain

Fig. 6.4
Probability Chain

Advantages of the Grapevine

- Social relations are built and the grapevine provides a high amount of psychological satisfaction to the employees. People come closer to each other and this builds organizational solidarity.
- Speed at which the messages are transmitted in the grapevine is unbelievable. Managers have been known to use the grapevine for their benefit to spread information through planned leaks.

- Support to other channels is given by the grapevine. Since all information cannot be sent across by official channels, hence the grapevine is used to supplement the official channel to transmit information that is not suitable for formal channels.
- Feedback also reaches the management very fast through the grapevine. This feedback can be useful to the organization.

Disadvantages of the Grapevine

- Distortion of the news is the major disadvantage of the grapevine; this channel of communication respects nobody and can destroy the image of even the noblest of the people.
- Rumor is the untrue part of the grapevine. Personal motives are usually dominant in the spread of news through the grapevine.
- Incomplete information is sometimes transmitted through the grapevine and thus a person cannot get a complete picture of any issue.
- Lack of authenticity is there in the news traveling through the grapevine as it is spread by word of mouth, and there are no tangible facts to support the news.

Effective use of the Grapevine

- The managers need to understand that the grapevine cannot be ignored and it will neither die nor wither and also that it can have damaging effects, therefore it is in the interest of the organization that the manager learns to use the grapevine effectively for the benefit of the organization.
- A manager should keep his ears and eyes open and try to spot the leaders and win their confidence.
- The management should let the employees be a part of the decision making process as far as possible. This helps the employees to feel

like being a part of a family.

- Rumors should be contradicted promptly and not wait till the harm is done.
- The organization is the source of bread and butter for its employees and nobody would like to harm the source if respect and dignity of all is maintained. Harmful rumors would automatically come to an end, and fruitful grapevine could be cultivated.
- Every manager needs to adopt an open door policy and maintain a healthy environment. A Manager needs be a good emphatic listener so that the employee feels free to talk to him rather than indulge in rumor mongering.
- The manager should use the grapevine for feedback and even try to improve any shortcomings that may be there in him as well as the management.
- Using the grapevine effectively can improve true productivity of the organization; therefore every manager should learn to do so.

Direction of Communication

As discussed earlier in this chapter, every organization has a hierarchical structure that may be compared to a pyramid. And communication in this organizational pyramid is multidirectional.

On the basis of the direction of the flow of communication, we classify it under four heads.

Downward Communication

Downward communication flows from the superiors to the subordinates. The main purpose is to communicate policies, objectives, programs circulars, orders, individual instructions, etc.

This forms the major chunk of the formal communications and usually the written part although verbal communication also happens.

Main Objectives of Downward Communication

- To give specific directions to the subordinates about

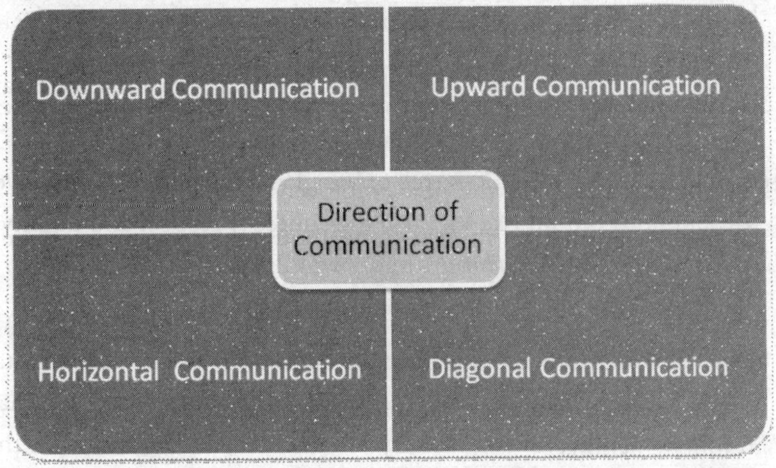

Fig. 6.5
Direction of Communication

what to do and how to do.

- To co-ordinate the working of various departments. This is a very important task in an organization. Various departments need to work in complete coordination with each other.
- To explain the organizational policies and procedures.
- To give Information to the subordinates about the rationale of their profile so that they are able to relate their profile with the organizational goals.
- To motivate the subordinates and thereby increase the productivity of the subordinates and hence the organization.
- To apprise the subordinates of their performance.

Media for Downward Communication

As discussed earlier, the downward communication may be both written and oral, although the written is more prominently used.

There are various modes or media, as we call them, used for the purpose.

- Annual reports are used to highlight facts pertaining to company finances, achievements, etc.

- Notices, posters etc carry the information about the activities in the organization and some miscellaneous information.
- Handbooks carry information especially for the new employees stating rules and policies of the organization.

This is for the orientation of the new employees.

- Pamphlets give the information about the organization, its services, products, etc.
- Journals, Newsletters etc also contain information about the organization about its various activities and achievements.
- Letters, e-mails, circulars, etc carry important directives required to imitate actions.
- Apart from the written communication, oral communication is also used as an important media for downward communication.

It is sometime much easier for a Managing Director to convene a meeting to pass on important information rather than using the written media.

But even in this case minutes of the meeting are usually recorded and again sent across to concerned people for further and future reference.

Advantages of Downward Communication

- Policies and plans are properly laid out and can be referred to whenever required.
- Mission and goals of the organization are set and the employees have the guidelines as to how best they can contribute to accomplish these goals.
- Every employee is aware of his duty and authority and also of what is expected from him.
- A sense of job satisfaction and a continuous motivation is there if the employees are regularly apprised of and appreciated for their good performance.

Limitations of Downward Communication

- Distortion or dilution occurs, quite often, of the

information originating at the highest level on its way to the base of the Organizational Pyramid.

- It may so happen that the messages get lost as well. Overstatement, under-statements, unconscious twist, etc also do happen.
- Under-communication and over communication also hiders and hampers the communication process.
- If too little is communicated, there are chances of unsatisfactory performance. And if too much is communicated then the chances of leaking out confidential information are there.
- Time consumption is a major limitation of downward communication.
- Sometimes the delay in the transmission of message from the top level to the lowest level is so that the message loses its significance.
- Filtering of information also occurs if the oral media has been used. And this prevents the entire message to move down in the hierarchical chain.
- An autocratic kind of a system sometimes, develops, wherein the subordinates do not get any chance of participation in the decision making process.

Hence a feeling of resentment and un-satisfaction build up and this can harm the organization.

Upward Communication

It signifies the flow of communication from the lower levels to the higher levels. The purpose of this type of communication is to send information, suggestions, complaints and grievances from the lower levels to the higher levels.

Earlier, this type of communication was not encouraged and it is only very recently that the managers have come to recognize the importance of upward communication.

Importance of Upward Communication

- Feedback received from the subordinates as a result of upward communication is very valuable. It helps the management to ascertain whether the order issued to the subordinates have been understood and followed or not.
- Also the feedback helps to know what the employees think of the organization and its policies.
- This kind of communication also allows the subordinates to give way to their pentup grievances and when heard patiently, the subordinate may feel happy and satisfied, that at least they have been heard and that something would be done in their favor.
- Upward communication helps to build better relations between the superiors and their subordinates and harmony at place of work means a successful and more productive environment.
- Valuable and constructive suggestions are often offered by the subordinates, which when implemented can prove to be fruitful for the organization.
- Upward communication helps to overcome resistance to change as well because there is freedom of communication and any fear or apprehension in the subordinate minds can be removed. Hence changes are welcomed.

Limitations of Upward Communication

- Distortion and filtering is more in upward communication than in downward communication. So if a 'level' feels the news may give an unfavorable picture to the seniors, it is edited or even distorted to one's own selfish motive.
- A feeling of fear and apprehension may be there in the minds of the subordinates and hence they would not pass on any news which they feel the superiors may not like.

- Not always does a boss like a subordinate to give him, his suggestions.
- There is an ego that may crop-up and hinder the effectiveness of communication. In such cases, the subordinate feels let down and morally depressed.
- Sometimes the subordinates become a little too bold and ignoring their immediate boss or superiors, they directly cut across the hierarchical line of command and approach the ones at the top. This also destroys the harmony at work and hence hampers the growth of the organization

Horizontal Communication

As the name suggests, the horizontal communication occurs between people working at he same level and status. It is also termed as lateral communication. The main purpose of this type of communication is to secure a harmonious co-ordination among the various departments.

For example:

An export company that has got an order cannot deliver it at the right time if the production department does not finish the production at the right time.

They can in-turn blame the purchase department for the delay in procuring the raw material.

The purchase department may throw the blame on to the finance department for not giving the payment in time, who may further put the blame on the liaison department for the delay in talking with the dealers and the blame finally falls on the marketing people for not giving enough time for the entire production process for such a huge order.

Hence until and unless, there is a proper coordination without any communication gap between various departments, it is not possible for the organization to achieve its targets and goals.

The chaotic situation may worsen if there be any conflicts between the departments.

Importance of Horizontal Communication

- Horizontal communication helps to create mutual understanding and develops trust and harmony amongst similar levels of different department in an organization.
- It helps to solve any conflicts that may occur and to create a harmonious environment.
- Horizontal communication facilitates problem solving and brings about better co-ordination between various departments.
- All interdepartmental and intradepartmental problems can be solved without the intervention of the management.

Limitations of Horizontal Communication

- There is a lack of authoritativeness as the ranks are the same. It is not as in downward communication wherein the acceptance is there because of the hierarchical authority.
- There may be an already existing rivalry between the same level people of different departments in an organization, and this is very common in today's era of fierce competition.
- Existing rivalries between departments also limit the communication and coordination amongst them.

Diagonal Communication

Communication between different levels belonging to different departments in an organization is called Diagonal Communication.

Sometimes cutting across the normal channel helps the organization but there are definitely some limitations as well.

Advantages of Diagonal Communication

- Helps in increasing the efficiency as cutting across normal levels helps to reduce the time factor.

- Also there can be better co-ordination and distortion or dilution of information can be avoided.
- Suppose there is a target at hand and the supervisor of the production department is facing a major IT problem. So instead of going through the normal hierarchical chain, he may directly approach the IT manager for help, although he may inform his immediate supervisor as well.

This way there is no delay and it is definitely more practical.

Limitations of Diagonal Communication

- Bypassing the immediate superior may disrupt the line of command and the superior may feel he has been sidelined.
- The superior may not co operate after he has been sidelined. It also may become a prestige issue.
- A chaotic situation may develop as frequent use of this channel leads to anarchy and animosity.

Test Yourself

1. What is the organizational pyramid?
2. What are the channels of communication?
3. Write a short note on the grapevine.
4. Discuss the various directions of communication.
5. Compare and contrast the advantages of upward and downward communication.

Chapter 7

Barriers to Communication

Learning Objectives

- To know the Barriers to Communication
- To understand how to Overcome the Barriers
- To study about SWOT analysis

Introduction to Barriers

The term 'Barrier means 'hindrance' or 'obstruction' hence, barriers in the communication process would be factors that hinder or hamper the effectiveness of the communication process.

These lead to confusion and chaos in the organizations because of the communication breakdown. There are quite a few reasons for this breakdown.

But before we go into the reasons, we need to understand that miscommunication can originate or occur at all the three levels of the transmission of the message: the sender, the media or the receiver.

Let us try to classify the barriers to have a better understanding of each. Because unless we understand how the barrier is distorting or destroying the Communication process, we shall not be able to remove them.

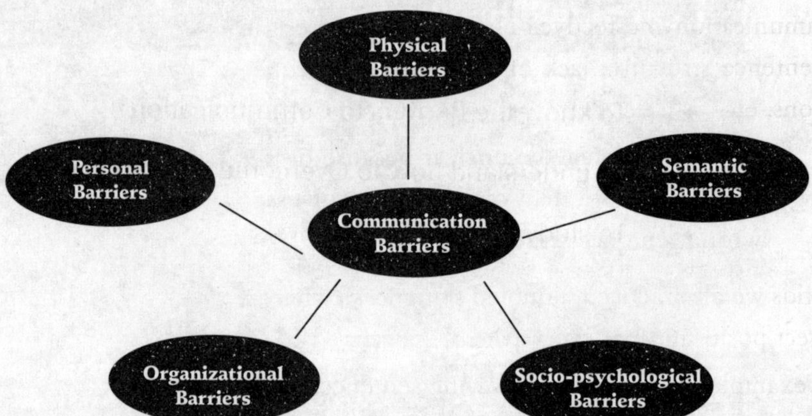

Fig. 7.1 Barriers

Physical Barriers

The physical or mechanical barriers may be caused by noise, time and distance and poor timing.

- Noise is quite often a barrier to communication, as communication can be effective only if there is NO noise to interfere. The Noise may be that of machines, traffic or even loud human sounds. It is important to understand that the word noise does not only refer to sounds.

- Noise may also be psychological in the form of ego clash, pre-occupied thought, fatigue, anxiety, etc.
- Time and distance also affect the effectiveness of a message or information.
- The receiver and the sender, if separated by a long distance find it difficult to communicate network add to the problem. Also there may be a communication gap between persons working in different shifts in the same organization.
- Poor timing of sending across a message may also result in reducing the effectiveness of the communication process, especially if the communication reaches too late.

Semantic Barriers

Language or Semantic barriers are other important factors that render communication ineffective. These include errors in the language, such as sentence structure, lack of coherence, inadequate vocabulary, use of jargons, etc.

- The message may be unclear because of the usage of words that may have more than one meaning, or usage of wrong words or wrong sentence structure.

As kids we all practiced 'jumbled sentences', wherein we were taught the correct positioning of every part of speech.

For example, consider the following sentences.

- I like to study only Business Communication.

  (Meaning I do not like any other subject)
- Only I like to study Business Communication.

(Meaning I am the only one who likes the subject)

- The Movie ended, happily.
- The Movie ended happily.

In the first example the position of the word only makes all the difference.

In the second example, the use of a comma has made all the difference of the meaning of the sentence.

- Misinterpretation of messages occurs when listeners interpret words based on personal definitions that have been established by background, education and experience.
- Denotations and Connotations may also hamper communication.

The literal meaning of a word is called its denotative meaning, where as connotative meanings arouse qualitative judgments and personal reactions.

Consider the example of the word 'cheap'. If a salesperson says that the products sold in the showroom are 'cheap'; we would not appreciate the word or the Salesperson, and probably leave the showroom without buying anything.

Therefore it is necessary to avoid problems associated with connotative meaning of word, as far as possible words with positive connotations should be used.

- The usage of jargon also may act as a barrier to communication. Jargon is technical language of a profession and obviously better understood by the people of the same profession. The usage of jargon elsewhere increases their isolation from others and hinders their communication with others.

Socio-Psychological Barriers

Factors like the Psychological needs and feeling of a person, place in society status in the hierarchical structure of the organization, differences in attitudes, family background, cultural differences, etc all are prime barriers in the communication process.

Let us look at some of these factors:

- Attitudes and opinions differ from person to person. Usually, people have a set mind and they welcome any information which might benefit them.

- However if they are of the opinion that a certain news may have an adverse effect on them they may reject it.
- Emotions also play a major role in the Communication process. If a person is already perplexed about an issue, he acts differently to a message, than he does if he were calm and happy.
- Prejudices are usually so deep-rooted in a person's mind, that he carries a closed mind and therefore is unable to be rational and this hinders the communication process.
- Status-consciousness can be a very serious barrier, especially in face-to-face communication.
- The overconfidence of a superior may lower the morale of an already under confident subordinate, hence hampering the communication process.
- Cultural diversity is yet another socio-psychological barrier to communication.
- Some gestures and etiquettes considered to be decent in one country may be considered highly offensive in another.

Hence in this globalized world, it is better to familiarize oneself of other cultures to avoid landing in an embarrassing situation.

- Family background, upbringing, education and experience also color the response of a person to a message.
- Lack of attention for any possible reason also hampers the communication process. The purpose is lost if the receiver is unable or unwilling to listen.
- Resistance to any change also acts as a barrier. This is because people feel that change makes things uncertain and threatens stability.

Organizational Barriers

Major organizational barriers are as follows.

- Status can be considered as an organizational barrier as well, because the hierarchical status sometimes changes the attitude of a person to another.

- In an organization, sometimes there is only one-way flow of communication. This happens when feedback from subordinates is restricted.

But we must always remember that communication can be effective only if it is a two-way flow.

- Rules and regulations also sometime restricts proper flow of information especially in public sector enterprises where observance of rules and regulations is more rigid, hence slowing down of the flow takes place, which in turn leads to delay in action.
- Filtering of information in both upward and downward flow of communication also acts as a barrier to communication.

Personal Barriers

Apart from the above factors, there are a lot may personal barriers to the process of communication.

- Attitude is one major problem in the communication process. If the Superior carries an attitude that is unfavorable, the flow of information gets hindered both from the superior and towards the superior.
- Lack of confidence in subordinates or overconfidence in superiors also, as discussed above, is a major personal barrier.

'The boss is always right', is a very famous line and explains the extent of being a major barrier.

- Lack of motivation, lack of incentives and a negative environment in an organization also build a barrier in the flow of information.

Overcoming the Barriers

For an organization, it is very necessary to have an effective communication system, both inside as well as outside. Hence it becomes necessary to overcome the above discussed barriers. Let us look at the various ways to overcome the barriers.

- Choose the right medium and right time for the information to be sent.
- Right kind of language or words should be used that may have a positive effect on the receiver.
- Cultural barriers should be understood carefully and avoided as well.
- 'Speak less, listen more', is a famous saying.

God has given you two ears and one mouth; hence use them in that order.

- Practice empathy and you can never go wrong.

Speak to others as you want others to speak to you.

Be courteous to all.

- Create a synergistic environment.
- Encourage open communication to encourage subordinates to come forward and discuss related to the goals of the organization.
- Ensure that there is a two-way communication.
- Communication can never be effective without a proper feedback system in place.

Therefore seek feedback and give clarification when ever required.

Overcoming barriers and ensuring effective communication can lead to organizational success which means prosperity to all.

SWOT

The term SWOT signifies as follows:

S ———————————— Strengths

W ———————————— Weaknesses

O ———————————— Opportunities

T ———————————— Threats

The organization uses the SWOT analysis to know the strengths and weaknesses of its communication network, be it formal or informal and exploit the opportunities to overcome the threats of today's globalised era of cut-throat competition.

The analysis can also be used by an individual to identify and overcome weaknesses.

To develop strategies for improvement of an individual or an organization based on SWOT analysis, a matrix of these can be constructed as shown below.

This matrix is also known as TOWS Matrix.

	Strengths	**Weaknesses**
Opportunities	S-O Strategies	W-O Strategies
Threats	S-T Strategies	W-T Strategies

- S-O strategies pursue opportunities that are a good fit to the company's strengths.
- W-O strategies help to overcome weaknesses to pursue opportunities.
- S-T strategies identify ways in which strengths may be used to overcome threats.
- W-T strategies help to establish plans to prevent weaknesses becoming susceptible to threats.

An organization may use the above strategies to create a harmonious and healthy environment to help the individual and organizational goals to be achieved.

Also, so that the organization is able to exploit the global markets and bring success to all associated with the organization.

Test Yourself

1. What are the various Barriers to Communication?
2. How can an organization overcome the barriers to be effective in the communication process?
3. Discuss SWOT.

Chapter 8

Effective Speech

Learning Objectives

- Introduction to an Effective Speech
- To understand the Characteristics of a Good Speech
- To enhance the art of Delivering a Speech

Introduction

How is it that some people can stir the minds of the Masses and motivate them to follow? It's all in the spoken word.

B. Jonson has rightly said, "Talking and eloquence are not the same; to speak and to speak well are two different things."

If you are familiar with the famous speech of Antony in 'Julius Ceaser', you would be able to recall that his speech was a master piece of oratory and full of rhetoric devices. He was able to accomplish his secret purpose of inciting the mob against the murderers of Julius Ceaser.

Similarly there have been many a famous speeches which have motivated people.

The key to success and fame of many political leaders, businessmen, salespersons, etc. lies in their capability to deliver an effective speech.

Characteristics of a Good Speech

Clarity

The foremost requisite of a good speech is clarity. The speaker should have both clarity of though and clarity of expression.
His language should be clear, and grammatically correct.

Conciseness

A good speech is one that does not go on and on. It should neither be too brief nor too long.

Ideally, a speech should not be more than fifteen to twenty minutes. It depends on the requirement and a speaker should adhere to the given time slot.

Informative

The audience would enjoy a speech that adds value to their knowledge. If the speaker is just beating around the bush, probably the audience would stop listening to him.

Informal

A speech need not be very formal unless of course the situation demands this.

A personal touch should be maintained because unless a rapport is established between the speaker and the audience, the purpose is not achieved.

Interesting

A good speech conveys concrete facts rather than abstract or vague ones.

Delivering a Speech

'A Good speaker is earnest'. A speech cannot be effective if not prepared properly.

A speaker needs to do some homework, as a speech cannot be cooked up, just a few minutes before its delivery.

However well informed a speaker may be, he/she needs to collect and organize his thoughts properly.

The next step is the delivery of the speech. The opening of the speech should be able to arouse the interest of the audience.

Well begun is half done!

Opening with a quotation can be very effective. The right kind of voice modulation is very essential for the speech to be effective. You may have written a very good speech but if your modulation is not effective, the entire effort is futile.

Eye contact is another important factor to make your speech, effective. The body language of the speaker is also important.

The ending of the speech should also be impressive. The speaker should summarize and outline briefly the main points.

And do not forget to compliment the audience for their patience. Closing with a fitting verse or biblical quotation also can add to the effectiveness of the speech.

Test Yourself

1. What are the characteristics of a good speech?
2. How can a speech be delivered effectively?

Chapter 9

Effective Presentation

Learning Objectives

- Introduction to an Effective Presentation
- To understand the Purpose of an Effective Presentation
- To study the Essential Features of a Good Presentation

Introduction

In today's competitive business world, the ability to deliver effective presentations is a much sought-after competence.

Business is about selling. It may be a product or a service, but it begins with a presentation, Sales happen, targets are achieved if the presentation is effective. On the other hand if the presentation is ineffective, sales fall even if the products or the services offered are better than others.

Presentation skills can be improved by understanding how an effective presentation can be delivered.

A presentation carries a speaker's personality along with it, hence you need to work on two aspects one, on the designing of the presentation, and two, on the personality of the speaker.

Fig. 9.1

Purpose of Presentation

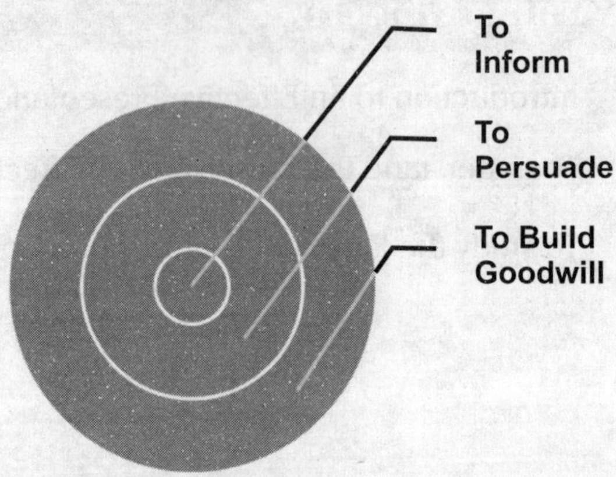

Purpose of Presentation

Oral presentations have the following three basic purposes.

To inform

This is the basic purpose of a presentation. To inform the audience about the products, services, schemes, etc. that the organization is offering. Hence the sales department always trains new sales persons about the organization and its products and services, before they enter into actual sales.

To persuade

Targets cannot be achieved unless sales happen. And sales cannot happen unless the buyers are persuaded to buy. And this persuasion is done through an effective presentation.

To build goodwill

An organization gives presentations to build its image and goodwill in the business world and among the general public as well.

Delivering an Effective Presentation

There are four main requirements for a successful and effective presentation.

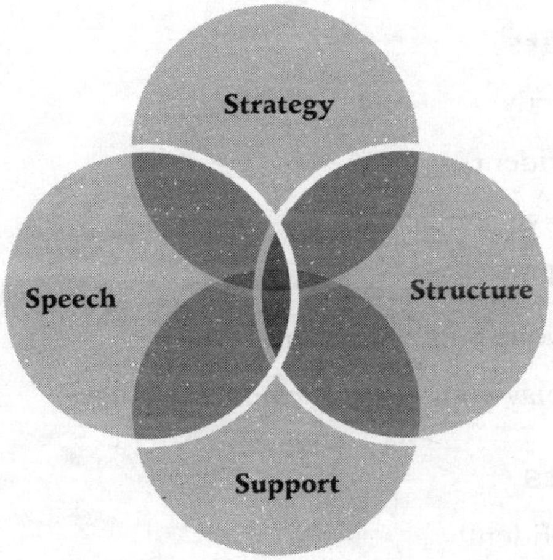

Fig. 9.2
Delivering an Effective Presentation

Strategy

The purpose of the presentation can help you to decide the strategy.

You should know your target audience, their economic and social status, their cultural background, their intellectual background, etc. Then only you can decide the location and the manner of persuading them.

Structure

Before a presentation is delivered, it needs to be structured.

Total information required for selling of the products or the services must be gathered and organized properly.

Logical sequencing should be given to the points, you wish to speak. Proper structuring can capture the attention of the audience, and persuade them to buy and BUY.

Support

Support can be the visual aids, charts, white boards, handouts, overhead projectors, LCD Projections, Video Tapes, etc.
These help in delivering a presentation effectively.

Speech

Speech is again a very important aspect of delivering an effective presentation. Recall the 7%-38%-55%. Rule discussed in the chapter 4, the same applies here.

Visual Elements

- Dress smartly.
- Look confident.
- Maintain eye contact.
- Avoid looking down at your notes.
- Work on your body language.
- Don't display your tension even if you have.

Vocal Elements

- Speak confidently.
- Modulate your voice.
- Don't be too loud or too soft.
- Work on the quality of your voice – the Pitch and the tone.
- Speak enthusiastically.
- Enjoy delivering your presentation, the audience will enjoy automatically.

Even after all the preparation and effort you put in, it may sometime happen that you make a mistake. But if you do, remember, the following lines.

'Know that even the best presenters make mistakes. The key is to continue after the mistake. If you pick up and continue, so will the audience.

Winners continue!

Losers stop!'

Test Yourself

1. Discuss the purpose of a presentation.
2. What are the essential features of an effective presentation?
3. Write a short note on the importance of speech in a presentation.

PART 2

THE BASICS OF CORRESPONDENCE

Chapter 10

Business Correspondence

Learning Objectives

- To get introduced to Business Correspondence
- To know the Importance of Business Correspondence

Introduction to Correspondence

In our day-to-day life, we exchange our feeling, ideas, thoughts and other information with our family, friends, relatives, business associates and other people.

This exchange is either verbal or nonverbal as discussed in the earlier chapters. When verbal, it may be either oral or written.

Correspondence is communication through exchange of written ideas, opinions, feelings, views, etc between family, friends, realties, business associates and other people.

When this type of communication takes place between business houses, businessmen, office etc, we call it Business Correspondence. And business correspondence may be related to matters of trade, commerce and industries.

All communication dealing with matters related to purchase and sale of goods, communication with suppliers and customers, etc in the form of letters is Business Correspondence.

Importance of Business Correspondence

Business Correspondence is an art and all business houses take special care in designing and writing letters they send across to their existing and prospective business associates.

Another important thing to remember is that business operations are not restricted to any locality, state or nation, in today's globalized world.

Today if production is one nation, the consumption may be world-wide. And obviously, it is impossible to contact every customer or retailer personally.

Thus, came up the need of letters. Business Correspondence was not essential in the past as trade was restricted but in today's business world, business letters have an increased importance because of the vast expansion and supply of goods and services.

Correspondence brings people, businessmen and nations closer to each other. Businesses cannot survive or flourish in this era, if effective and purposeful correspondence does not exist.

Let us understand the importance of business correspondence.

a) Helps in maintaining proper business relationships.

As discussed above, business activities are not confined to one locality, state or nation. We need to build business relations world-wide.

Thus, comes up the need of business correspondence which helps to contact and maintain relationship with existing and prospective business associates and customers.

The customers may seek information through letters. Thus business may be carried on a national and an international basis.

b) A convenient and inexpensive mode of communication.

STD and ISD calls cost a lot and hence business letters are a more convenient and inexpensive mode of sending and receiving information however lengthy it may be.

c) A business letters is a record.

It is not possible to remember or memorize all facts and figures in an oral conversation.

However, the written correspondence helps to record all communication in a business. And records are easy to help recall the earlier communication, when maintained properly.

d) Business correspondence serves as evidence.

Any record that has been received or sent can be used as legal evidence if the need arises.

These may be produced in court, if a dispute arises between two parties.

e) Useful for future reference.

Again, if records are maintained properly, the same may be useful for future reference.

Recorded business correspondence helps to plan, in a better way, all future dealings.

f) Helps to create and maintain goodwill.

Business houses today incur high expenses in creating and maintaining goodwill. A good image is the key to success.

It is very important to maintain cordial relations with the customers to survive in today's market of cut throat competition. Customers need to be updated regularly about the new product launched by the company, a clearance sale, etc.

Business correspondence is also helpful in thanking the customers for their support and loyalty to the products and services of the company.

Test Yourself

1. Correspondence is the key to success for a business'. Comment.
2. Discuss the importance of Business Correspondence.

Chapter 11

Business Letters

Learning Objectives

- To know the Important Features of a good Business Letter
- To study the Parts of a Business Letter
- To understand the Layout of Letters

Important Features of a Good Business Letter

A business letter is much different from other kinds of letters that we read or write in its content, format and features.

Above all it should serve the purpose for which it is written. There are some important or essential features of a business letter, and care should be taken in writing one, so as to avoid any miscommunication or incomplete communication.

Following are the features of good business letters:

Clarity

A business letter should be written in a lucid and clear language so that the receiver is able to understand what the sender wishes to convey.

Ambiguous language should be avoided at all costs, so that the meaning is clear. A good correspondent should be able to organize the information in a clear, correct, logical and impressive manner.

Confusing the customer hampers business relationships.

Simplicity

Using words for which the receiver need to turn pages of a dictionary world not help the business but put-off the customer.

Hence business letters should be written in correct but simple and lucid language.

Accuracy

All facts and figures mentioned in a business letter should be accurate. Remember that any false statements may lead to loss of business and even legal action in extreme cases.

Accuracy also implies that the language written is grammatically correct. Errors in written correspondence are never appreciated.

Completeness

Business letters should be able to provide all information that is necessary for the receiver to know or which the sender wants the receiver to be aware of.

Incomplete information is never appreciated and the customer may feel that the company is hiding facts on purpose.

And if the letter is from the customer to the company and the information regarding an order is incomplete, it will lead to a delay in the delivery.

Conciseness

Time is very precious, for the receiver as well as the sender. Hence a business letter should be concise but not at the cost of completeness and clarity.

Unnecessary repetition should be avoided as lengthy letters are not appreciated; in fact they irritate a receiver.

Relevance

Only information that is relevant should be written in a business letter. There is no room for irrelevant details hence should be avoided.

Courtesy

However formal, but a business letter should also be courteous, respectful and sensitive.

Courtesy wins the heart of the reader. Dignity of business should be maintained at all costs. Being rude and discourteous never helps even if there is a dispute to be settled.

Convincing power

The purpose of a business letter is to expand business, which means to win customers. Hence a business letter should be highly convincing.

A correspondent should have a very good power of expression so that he/she creates a letter that is impressive, effective and of course convincing.

The power of persuasion of the correspondent is clear from a letter.

Neatness

An untidy letter irritates the receiver. A good business letter whether handwritten or typed, should be neat and attractive.

Untidy paper, overwriting and cutting should be avoided.

Apart from the essential features discussed above, there are quite a few features that relate to the outer qualities of a letter. They are as follows:

- Quality of paper used reflects the economic status of the organization. Care should be taken in selecting the right kind of paper.
- Size of the paper is usually the standard A4 size. And this is convenient, for both the receiver and the sender, for filing purpose.

If a receiver gets different sizes of letters from different firms, he would find it difficult to file them.

Folding of the letter

The folding of the letter should be done with utmost care, giving it minimum folds so that it looks neat and also fits in the envelope that is being used. The folds should be uniform and neat and refolding again and again to fit the envelope should be avoided.

Envelope

The letter is written impressively and folded neatly, but what if the envelop used is not proper.

The entire effort of creating a good business letter is wasted. Hence care should be taken in selecting a good quality and right sized envelop to add the good qualities of the letter inside it.

Receiver's name and address should be either typed or written very neatly.

Parts of a Business Letter

A business letter has a different format from the other types of letter.

There are some essential features, which have been discussed earlier in this chapter.

Now let us look at the essential parts of a business letter, without which it would not look like a business letter.

The essential parts of a business letter are as follows:

Heading

The heading of a business letter includes the name and postal address of the business, E-mail address, Web-site address, Telephone Number, Fax Number and Trade Mark or logo of the business (if any).

Firms prefer to use printed letter heads these days. Many firms prefer to put much of the above information at the bottom of the letterhead, where we call it letter foot. This basically saves the top of the page from looking cluttered. But the firm's name should always be at the top.

The name and address of the firm are usually at the centre of the page, although the address may be optionally given at the right side of the page.

While writing the address, if the building number or the lane number is being mentioned then no comma is required after it.

The main purpose is to make the letterhead as neat and impressive as possible.

The Date

The date is normally written on the right hand side corner below the heading, although it is sometimes typed or written close to the left margin as well.

There is a proper format for writing a date as well. Any of the following may be used:

15th May, 20--

Or

15 May, 20--

Or

May 15, 20—

It is necessary, while writing the date, to avoid using abbreviations and cutting short the year as '09 or '10.

Reference

The reference number indicates the letter number allotted to it. It helps in future reference and correspondence.

This is a very important number especially where a large volume of correspondence is being handled.

Reference number is given on the left hand corner after the heading usually opposite to the 'date' and in the same line.

Inside Address

The inside address includes the name and full address of the person or the firm to whom the letter is addressed. This is written on the left hand side below the reference number.

The name of the receiver should be prefixed with courtesy titles. If the letter is to an individual then add Ms., Mrs. or Mr. and if the letter is to a firm, then it should be addressed to the responsible head, e.g., the secretary, the chairman, etc.

In case the letter is to a firm and no particular head is known, then add 'messrs or M/S'.

For example:

M/S Nisha Enterprises
Nisha Complex
51, Nehru Place
New Delhi -110019

Or

Ms. Nisha Chopra
Nisha Enterprises
Nisha Complex
51, Nehru Place
New Delhi -110019

The inside address is exactly similar to the one written on the envelope.

Subject

It is customary to state in brief the subject of the letter. It is given to attract the attention of the receiver immediately and enable him to understand what the letter is understand what the letter is about.

If any reference has to be made to a previous letter, then it is also mentioned.

For example:

Subject: Your order No. D124 dated March 10, 2009.

The subject is written or typed either on the left side below the inside address or five spaces away from the left margin so that it stands out prominently from the rest of the parts.

Salutation

Salutation is a way of greeting to the receiver. It is written below the inside address next to the left margin.

The words to be used for salutation depend on whom the letter is addressed to.

For example:

Sir or Madam	For official correspondence with Government Departments.
Dear Sir or Dear Madam	This is the most commonly used salutation for a business letter to a businessman or a businesswoman.
Dear Mr. Kant or Dear Mrs. Kant	This type of salutation is used if you are familiar with the receiver.

The salutation may or may not end with a comma.

Body of the letter

This comes after the salutation.

The body of the letter is the most important part and the most difficult to write as well.

It is to be divided into three paragraphs.

- Opening paragraph or the introductory paragraph
- Main part or the main body
- Concluding part or the closing part

The opening or the introductory part deals with the message of the letter and reference to any previous correspondence. This paragraph should attract the attention of the receiver such that he feels inclined to read the entire letter with full concentration and interest.

If you fail here, the purpose is lost. Never begin your letter with stereotyped openings. The purpose of this part is to arrest the interest of the receiver.

The main paragraph is the longest part of the letter and therefore should be very carefully written to avoid language errors and monotony. Care should be taken to avoid ambiguous words and that no relevant details are left out. A draft of the same must be prepared and edited carefully before a final copy is made.

The concluding part or closing paragraph is as important as the opening one. It should flow naturally from the main part towards a conclusion.

The purpose is to motivate the receiver for an action that the sender wants. The language must be friendly yet forceful, gentle yet firm.

Conclusion should be done on a positive note. At the end, terms like thanking you, with warm regards should be used.

Complimentary close

This is a formal yet polite way of closing the body of the letter using respectful phrases. Complimentary close or subscription as we generally call it must be in accordance to the salutation that has been used.

Let us see how it may be written.

Salutation	Subscription	Remarks
Dear Sir Dear Sirs Dear Madam Dear Mesdames	Yours faithfully	The most common formal subscription for business letters.
Dear Sir Dear Sirs Dear Madam Dear Mesdames	Yours truly	Less formal, used between persons who are acquainted with each other.
Sir Gentlemen Madam Mesdames	Yours respectfully	To be used while addressing superiors
Dear Mr. Suraj Dear Ms. Nisha	Yours sincerely	To be used between persons known to each other. This is used very commonly in business letters to show informal relations.

Signature

Even if the entire letter is typed, the signature is usually hand-written and should be legible.

Below the signature, the name and designation of the sender are typed.

For example:

Yours faithfully

(Signature)

Yash Chopra

Head-Marketing

Or

Yours faithfully

For M/S Chopra & Sons

(Signature)

Yash Chopra

Head-Marketing

Enclosures

Quite often there may be documents to be sent along with a letter. The documents may be a cheque, a draft, bills, receipts, invoices, order forms, etc.

In such a case, the mention of the documents should be done in the letter as well, after the signature near the left hand margin.

For example:

Encls: Two

Or

Encl: 1) A cheque for Rs. 10,000 (Ten Thousand Only) drawn on PNB.

2) A copy of the order from.

Even in the case of no enclosures, it is customary to mention as follows:

Encl: NIL.

Copy Circulation

This is required when copies of a letter are to be sent to some other people as well apart of the actual receiver.

They may be marked as follows:

C.C Mr. Kant

Or

C.C The Manager, XYZ Company.

Post – Script (P.S.)

P.S. (Latin Postscriptum) is required when the writer wishes to add something in the body of the letter.

This is also used to convey some important information but in a line.

The person who has signed the letter must sign again otherwise P.S. is meaningless.

For example:

P.S. My heartiest felicitations on your assuming the charge of the department (Signature)

Or

P.S. – We provide 2- year On-site warranty. (Signature)

Reference initials

These days it is customary to type the initials of two people, the first who has dictated the letter and the second, who has typed the letter.

This is done towards the end of the letter and close to the left hand margin.

For example:

R.K. / S.K.

This explains that RK has dictated the letter and SK has typed it.

Layout Of Letters

A business as discussed above needs to be typed in a particular manner that is conventionally determined. The conventional system is followed to avoid confusion and waste of time as the business world is used to a particular format.

The different layouts are as follows:

Full-block format

This is a very popular format and is widely used. This is what we refer to as the left aligned letter.

All parts of the letter are left aligned except the date which may be right aligned, the Name of the company that is centre aligned and the address of the company may be either at the centre along with the name or near the right hand margin.

Also important is the fact that an open pattern of punctuation is used, which means that only essential marks are used outside the body of the letter since every part is left aligned, no typing adjustment are required, hence this format helps save time.

Full-block Format

Telephone: ____________ Telegram: ____________

Post Box No.:__________ Telex: ______________

1. Name of Sender

(Details of Business)

Address

____

____

____

2. Ref.: ____________ 3. Date: ________

4. Inside Address

____

____

____

5. Sub : ____________

Ref: ____________ (Receiver's reference)____

6. Salutation ____________

7. Introductory Para ________________________________

____

____

____

Main Body

____

____

____

Closing Para ____________________________________

____

____

____

8. Complimentary close

Sd/-

(Name)

9. Designation

For: ____________

10. Encl. 1. ______________

2. ______________

11. Initials of Dictator and Typist

12. Copy to: 1. ______________

2. ______________

3. ______________

Full Indent Format

In this method, the parts are typed in different margins, usually five spaces indented.

This, obviously, consumes a let of time for typing and hence is avoided.

Telephone: ________ Telegram: "______________"

Post Box No.:____________ Telex: ____________

2. Name of Sender

(Details of Business)

Address

____

____

____

2. Ref.: ______________ 3. Date: ______________

4. Inside Address

____

____

____

5. Sub : ____________________

Ref: ________________ (Receiver's reference)____________

6. Salutation ________________

7. Introductory Para ____

____

____

____

Main Body ____

____

____

____

____

____

Closing Para ____

____

____

____

8. Complimentary close

Sd/-

(Name)

9. Designation

For: ______________

10. Encl. 1. ____________________

2. ____________________

11. Initials of Dictator and Typist

12. Copy to: 1. ____________________

2. ____________________

3. ____________________

Modified Block Format

This format is similar to the full block format, although some parts in the full indent format.

This is also widely used method in our country especially in government offices.

This letter format also is a time saver. No comma marks are used after the salutation or the subscription.

Telephone: ________________

Mobile No.:_______________

Name of Sender

(Details of Business)

Address

____

____

____

Ref.: ______________________

Date: _____________________

Inside Address

____

____

____

____

Subject: ___________________

Salutation ________________

Introductory Para ____

____

____

____

Main Body ____

____

____

____

____

____

Closing Para ____

____

____

____

____

____

____

Complimentary close

Sd/-

(Name)

Designation

For: ______________

Encls. 1. __________________

2. __________________

Copy to: 1. __________________

2. __________________

3. __________________

Initials of Dictator and Typist:

Test Yourself

- Explain the essential features of a good business Letter
- What are the parts of a business letter?

Chapter 12

Types of Letters

Learning Objectives

- To learn about the different Types of Business Letters
- To understand what is an Enquiry Letter
- To study a Quotation Letter
- To study a Order Letter
- To study a Complaint Letter
- To study a Recovery Letter

Types Of Business Letter

After having an idea about the various essential qualities and different parts of a good business letter, let us discuss about the different types of letter used in business correspondence.

Business letters are written for the fulfillment of several purposes. The purpose may be to enquire about a product to know its price and quality, availability, etc. This purpose is served if you write a letter of enquiry to the supplier.

After receiving your letter the supplier may send you details about the product as per your requirement.

You may then give an order for supply of goods as per your requisition.

These are the few instances in which business correspondence takes place.

Let us study the details about some important business letters.

Business Enquiry Letter

Sometime prospective buyers wish to know the details of the goods which they want to buy, like quality, price, mode of delivery and payment etc.

They may also ask for a sample. The letter that is written to sellers with one or more of the above purposes is known as an enquiry letter.

Specimen of Business Enquiry Letter

Tel. 011-29292929 M/s M. Electricals e-mail: m.elec@gmail.com

Fax: 28282828 29, Main GT Road Website: http://www.m.elec.com

Chandni Chowk Delhi-6

Ref.PA/F/2008/27 Date: July 27, 2008

M/s Usha Generators

Usha Complex

Udaipur Industrial Estate

Udaipur –32

Subject : Enquiry about the prices of generators

Dear Sir,

We are dealing in retail trade of industrial electrical Goods. We would be interested in selling your product, 5KVA-20KVA Generators through our retail showroom.

Could you, therefore, send us your quotations and let us know the terms and conditions of payment.

Thanking You,

Yours faithfully,

For M/s M. Electricals

Sd/-

(N.K.Mishra)

Proprietor.

There are a few things to be kept in mind while writing letters of enquiry-

- Letters of enquiry should clearly state the information required, which may be asking for a pricelist or a sample.
- Mention specifically about the design, size, quantity, quality, etc. about the product or service in which you are interested.

Quotation Letter

After receiving the letter of enquiry from a prospective buyer, the sellers supply the relevant information by writing a letter that is called quotation letter.

These letters are written keeping in view the information asked for like price list, mode of payment, discount to be allowed etc.

Businessman should reply to the inquiries carefully and promptly.

Specimen of Quotation Letter

Tel. Name & Address e-mail:

Fax:

Ref.SL/F/2009/12 Date: August 10, 2009

M/s M.Electricals

Subject: Your letter No. ------------Dated ----------

Dear Sir,

Thanking you for your letter of enquiry. We would be glad to meet your requirements of selling our generators in your retail outlet.

Our quotations are given in the prices list enclosed. We offer 15% discount on order above Rs. --------, besides, we allow a grace period of 45 days for payment of dues to our regular customer.

We are confident that you will find our prices competitive and our terms and conditions reasonable. We look forward to meeting your requirements.

Thanking You,

Yours faithfully,

For M/s -----------

Sd/-

(---------------)

Designation

Encl : Price List & Terms and Conditions

Order Letter

The prospective buyer after receiving the reply to his enquiry letter may decide to place on order with that business house which offers goods at minimum price and at favorable terms and conditions.

Thereafter, a letter is written by a buyer to the seller giving the order to purchase the goods in called order letter.

Specimen of Order Letter

Tel. 011-29292929 M/s M. Electricals e-mail: m.elec@gmail.com

Fax: 28282828 29, Main GT Road Website: http://www.m.elec.com

Chandni Chowk Delhi-6

Rcf.PA/F/2008/27 Date: August 17, 2008

Subject: Your letter of quotation No. --------dated August 10, 2009

Dear Sir,

Many thanks for your prompt replay to our enquiry letter of July 27, 2009. As we find your prices and terms quite reasonable, we wish to place a trial order as per the list enclosed.

As pointed out in our enquiry letter, quality is important. Should the goods meet our expectations, substantial order will follow.

Payment will be made within the time limit prescribed in your quotation letter.

Thanking You,

Yours faithfully,

For M/s --------

Sd/-

(Name)

Designation

Complaint Letter

A complaint letter is written when the purchaser does not find the goods up to his satisfaction.

It is normally written by the purchaser when he receives defective or damaged goods or receives incorrect quantity of goods, it can also be written directly to the transit authority when the goods are damaged in transit.

Thus, we may define a letter of complaint as the letter that draws the attention of the supplier or any other party on account of supply of defective or damaged goods.

Points to be considered while writing a complaint letter-

- Complaint letters should be written immediately after receiving the defective goods.
- Suggestions on how the complaint should be dealt with i.e., mention of compensation, replacement, etc, should be made.
- Mention period in which the corrective action should be taken
- Request to be more careful in future.

Specimen of Complaint Letter

Tel. 011-29292929 M/s M. Electricals e-mail: m.elec@gmail.com

Fax: 28282828 29, Main GT Road Website: http://www.m.elec.com

Chandni Chowk Delhi-6

Ref.----------------- Date: September10,2008

Ref.------------------- Date: September10,2009

M/s Name

Address

Subject : Complaint regarding Generators

Dear Sir,

I would like to draw your attention to the fact that 3 out of 5 Generators are found defective, dispatched by you, which I received today. It appears that all the generators were not checked properly before dispatching.

We will appreciate if the three generators are replaced as soon as possible.

Yours faithfully,

For M/s ----------------

Sd/-

(name)

Designation.

Recovery Letter

The letter written by the seller for collection of money for the goods supplied to the buyer is called recovery letter. The aim of a recovery letter is to collect money without annoying the customer.

The letter should include information regarding the amount of arrears. The most important thing to remember is that the language of the recovery letter should be polite; so that the customer is does not feel offended and future transactions with him are not adversely affected because nobody wants sales to happen only once.

Specimen of Recovery Letter

Tel. 011-29292929 M/s M. Electricals e-mail: m.elec@gmail.com

Fax: 28282828 29, Main GT Road Website: http://www.m.elec.com

Chandni Chowk Delhi-6

Ref.----------------- Date: September10, 2008

M/s ---------------

Address----------

Subject: Recovery of dues

Dear Sir,

We believe that the payment of our bill no. ---------Dated ----------must have escaped your attention. As the payment is due since long, we would appreciate if you send us your cheque immediately.

Please let us know whether payment is being withheld for some special reasons.

Thanking You,

Yours faithfully,

For M/s ----------

Sd/-

(-------------)

Manager

Test Yourself

1. What is an enquiry Letter?
2. What is the difference between a quotation letter and an order letter?
3. What points do you need to keep in mind for writing a complaint Letter?
4. What is a recovery Letter?

Chapter 13

Writing a Cover Letter

Learning Objectives

- To know the Importance of a Cover Letter
- To understand the Purpose of a Cover Letter
- To know the Guidelines to Write a good Cover Letter
- To study the Essential Features of a Cover Letter
- To know the Types of the Cover Letter

Importance of a Cover Letter

The cover letter you send with your resume initiates contact with the person who holds the power to hire you. The HR manager who receives hundreds of letters and resumes often must make snap decisions based on an instant's evaluation: Does this applicant potentially have the background we're looking for?

As your opening communication, your cover letter creates the first impression about you. A vague and ineffective letter conveys a negative impression-and stacks the deck against you.

The Cover letter that communicates well leaves a good impact on the HR Manager. As you seek to market yourself, your ability to articulate your values to the employer's organization may spell the difference between a door slammed shut and an interview that is your first step to a satisfying career.

The cover letter, therefore, is one of the most important letters you ever write.

Think of the total income you will receive, if you're hired, over the course of your employment with this organization. Isn't it worth taking time to craft the best letter you can, if it stands a chance of increasing your prospects of landing the position?

Many people invest substantial time in developing their resumes, but skimp on the cover letter. Why risk being eliminated from consideration by a hastily prepared letter, poor letter design, grammatical errors, and misspelled words.

A resume without a cover letter fires a shot in the dark. Without a cover letter, you appear to be sending resumes randomly and mechanically. Is a mass mailing likely to communicate your particular interest in that specific employer's organization? It is very important for the organization to know that you are eagerly interested to join them.

Further, you miss an opportunity to convey some important information that doesn't fit easily into the resume.

Remember you need to cast the Best First Impression.

The Purpose of a Cover Letter

Before you begin working on your cover letter, it's important that you understand its purpose. A well-written cover letter achieves several purposes that are usually not accomplished by the resume alone.

Let us look at the various purposes of a cover letter:

- Introduces you and your credentials to the prospective employer.
- Highlights reasons for your interest in the company and the position.
- It is a kind of sales letter that tells why you are particularly qualified for that specific job. Remember you are trying to market yourself.
- Establishes a more personal connection with a prospective employer in a way that the resume cannot.
- Provides a glimpse of your unique personality and tries to prove your suitability.
- A good cover letter would stimulate interest in meeting you for a personal interview.

Guidelines to Write a Good Cover Letter

Before you read the guidelines remember you need to do your best in crafting the best Cover Letter you can. This is your first introduction to the organization. Hence make them want to meet you. Remember you want them more than they want you. But you need to change this to they want you.

- Follow the accepted format for writing a business letter.
- Format your letter on one page, typed, and single-spaced.
- Edit your letter before you send it across to be sure that it is grammatically correct and that there are no spelling errors.

- Address the letter to a specific person, rather than to the attention of the personnel or human resources department.
- Avoid using terms like, 'To Whom It May Concern'.
- Don't guess at gender. If you're not sure, use the person's entire name, for example, 'Dear Kelly Jones' instead of 'Mr. or Ms.' Or 'Dear Sir or Madam.'
- Be original. You must read sample letters but do not copy.
- Compose the introductory paragraph in a way that compels the reader to continue reading.
- Capture the interest of the reader by displaying your interest in the company and the industry.
- Emphasize what you can contribute to the organization, not what they can do for you. Every company is looking forward to employing people who can add value to the company.
- Express enthusiasm and self-confidence but yet show humility as well. The basic idea is never display overconfidence.
- If you are required to mail your resume, the cover letter should be the body of the email and the resume should be included as an attachment.
- Be patient, polite, and persistent in your follow-up.

Essential Features of a Cover Letter

You should adopt a conservative format and focus on content that communicates your qualifications and interest.

The letter should have a format that is being used commonly in the Business environment and the formats have been already discussed in the earlier chapter.

The letter and resume should be mailed in a No. 10 business

envelope with return address typed in the upper left corner, recipient's address typed in the centre of the envelope.

Let us look at the features that are considered essential for the purpose:

The Essential features of The Cover Letter

Return Address :	Your Address City, State, Zip Date of Letter
Inside Address :	Contact's Name Contact's Title Company Name Street Address City, State, Zip
Salutation Opening Paragraph :	Dear Mr./Ms. (Contact's Last Name): Capture attention ; establish match Statement of where you are now, what job you are interested in and why you are interested in this particular company
Body Paragraph :	Explain qualifications; create interest; encourage attentive review: An overview of your competencies (knowledge, attitudes, skills, habits) and unique strengths, stated in terms of the unique value you bring to teams and organizations Discuss the positive results you achieved in previous or educational contexts.

Closing :	Sincerely (3-4 lines for signa ture) Type full Name
Enclosure(s):	Resume (always); other supporting documents (occasionally)

Please always keep in mind that cover letters should not be mass-produced. You may, however, develop a core document that talks about your strengths, abilities, competencies, and market value, Beyond that, each letter should be TAILOR MADE.

Types of Cover Letters

Solicited or Invited Letters

This includes cover letters that respond to classified ads in newspapers, journals, and online postings.

This would also include letters in response to jobs posted by companies in recruiting interviewing on campus that pre-select students to interview.

Solicited or invited letters should always be tailored to the specific requirements of the job for which you are applying.

Unsolicited/Targeted Letters

These letters have a broader marketing approach designed to tap the hidden recipients.

Letters are sent to contacts at your targeted list of companies from commercial databases, books, directories, newspaper and trade journals and company literature etc.

Referral Letters

Referral letters use names of people you know or names of people you've met or obtained through networking.

If your contact is someone the employer knows, mention the name of the contact to get the employer's attention. But remember always to be sure to get the person's permission for you to use his or her name.

Test Yourself

1. What is the importance and purpose of a cover letter?
2. What are the basic guidelines for writing a cover letter?
3. Discuss the essential features of a cover letter.

Chapter 14

Notice, Agenda & Minutes

Learning Objectives

- To understand 'a Notice'
- To understand 'the Agenda'
- To understand 'the Minutes'

Introduction

Every organization conducts meetings regularly for various purposes. The meetings are usually planned properly, a notice is sent to all required to attend along with the agenda of the meeting.

The agenda helps all attending the meeting to understand the need of the meeting and everyone is ready with their homework done.

The minutes of the meeting are recorded and then sent across to all who attended.

Let us look at all three – Notice, Agenda & Minutes one by one.

Notice

A notice is circulated to all those who are entitled or required to attend the meeting.

It is in writing and is given well in advance. The notice also gives the date, time and venue of the meeting. It also specifies as to why a meeting has been called. The notice is signed by a person competent to call the meeting.

Let us look at some specimen.

Notice 1

Notice to warn the public against dealing with a particular person.

PUBLIC NOTICE

This is to inform the general public that Mr. Sanjeev Kapoor, Manager – Marketing Division, has been suspended on account of fraud. Anybody dealing with him will do so on his own risk.

Date: March 10, 2009

Sd/-

General Manager

Chopra Motors

2, Darya Ganj

Delhi –110006.

Notice 2

Notice to the Managers of all departments for a meeting with the M.D.

CHOPRA MOTORS

2, Darya Ganj, Delhi – 110006

Date: March 10, 2009

NOTICE FOR MEETING

This is to inform the Managers of all departments that the M.D. has called for a meeting to discuss the targets for the next financial year.

The meeting has been scheduled for March 15, 2009 at 11:30 am in the conference Room.

Sd/-

Mr. A. Gupta

General Manager

Agenda

Agenda as discussed above gives the contents of a forthcoming meeting and is usually sent along with the notice. The persons required to attend the meeting can therefore be ready for the meeting and do any homework that may be required.

Sometimes the agenda is unknown to all till the meeting begins, and hence only the notice is circulated and that too without any agenda or purpose of the meeting.

Let us look at a specimen.

CHOPRA MOTORS

2, Darya Ganj, Delhi-110006

Agenda for the meeting to be held in the Conference Room on March 15, 2009 at 11:30 a.m.

- To look back and discuss the targets of 2008-2009.
- To appreciate the achievers.
- To discuss and set targets for the next financial year i.e. 2009-2010.

Mr. Gupta

General Manager

Minutes

By 'Minutes' we mean an official record of a meeting that has been held. The points discussed, issues raised and decisions taken are all recorded in a concise and accurate manner.

The minutes are very helpful in the future and are always recorded and filed properly.

They carry the signature of the authority who had called the meeting. He verifies and then signs and may act as prima-facie evidence in case a dispute arises.

They are generally not written in narrative form. Minutes record the date, time and venue of the meeting. The name of the presiding officer and the agenda are also recorded.

The minutes are recorded as soon as possible after the meeting.

There are two kinds of minutes:-

Minutes of Resolution

In minutes of resolution, only passed resolutions are recorded and there is no reference to any discussion that was held preceding the resolution. Each paragraph begins with the word 'Resolved'.

Minutes of Narration

In minutes of narration, in addition to the resolutions passed, an account of the discussion, preceding the resolution, is also included.

Specimen of minutes of resolution

Resolved that the incentives for the achievers of 2008–2009 be released before the end of this financial year.

Further resolved that the targets for each zone be increased by 20% and the incentives by 50%.

There being no other item on the agenda, the meeting ended with a vote of thanks to the chair.

Dated: March 15, 2009 Sd/-

Sd/-

G.M. M.D.

Test Yourself

1. Discuss the importance of a Notice.
2. What is agenda?
3. What are minutes of a meeting? Why are they prepared?

Chapter 15

Report Writing & Press Release

Learning Objectives

- To know what is Report Writing
- To understand the Importance of Report Writing
- To understand the Essential Features of a good Report
- To study about the Principles of Drafting a Report
- To know the Format of a Report
- To understand what is a Press Release
- To know about the Essential Features of a good Press Release

Report Writing

A report is a formal statement related to an event or some activity. It contains a detailed account of a problem or a situation, findings of an investigation, recommendations or action taken and suggestions for future course of action.

Importance

It is easy for a proprietor to take decisions on the spot as and when required, because he knows his business inside out. But in large organizations, this is not possible. Hence arises the need for reports as they can help in analyzing a situation and suitable action plan can be taken up. Thus, we can say that reports are an important tool used in the decision making process.

Reports help the management to review and evaluate all operations in an organization regularly.

They can also help to measure the performance of various departments in the organization. Hence they can help to assess the effectiveness of the organization as a whole. Reports analyze situations and through the recommendations, they help to bring about changes in business policies.

Essential Features of a Good Report

Accuracy

A good report should always be accurate and give an unbiased opinion. Only then correct decisions can be taken.

Simplicity

A good report must be in a very simple and lucid language. This is required so that it is understood by all who read it otherwise the purpose or writing the repot is lost.

Clarity

Clarity of thought and clarity of expression is required to write a good report. The writer should have a clear purpose, clear findings and recommendations.

The report should be presented in a logical and attractive manner. It should be divided into short paragraphs with suitable headings and sub-headings so that the report gives a neat look and not an over cluttered look.

Consistency

The report should be consistent with its purpose and not deviate from the main theme.

Completeness

A good report is complete in all respects. No important details, facts and conclusions are left out.

Objectivity

There has to be objectivity in observation, collection of facts and writing of reports. The final report should present all facts, in an unbiased manner. It should not be colored by personal grudges or prejudices.

Conciseness

Although, we require a report which has all relevant data, but it should be concise.

Nobody has the time to read very lengthy reports, hence it should be brief, but of course not at the cost of clarity and completeness.

Relevance

A report should be relevant to its purpose and no facts that may make the report misleading or obscure should be added.

Timelines

The purpose of the report is lost if it is not prepared well in time.

Reader-oriented

While preparing a report, the reader should be kept in mind. Usage of jargon and very high level of vocabulary will never help to achieve its purpose.

The reader may be a layman, hence it should be in a language that is understandable by all.

Principles of Drafting a Report

Principle of Purpose

Every report must have a clear purpose.

Principle of Organization

The report should be properly and logically organized.

Principle of Clarity

There should be clarity of expression and the language should be lucid.

Principle of Conciseness

The report should not be lengthy. It should give all relevant facts in a concise manner to help save time and cost.

Principle of Scheduling

The report should be prepared and circulated well in time. The purpose is lost if there is a delay.

Principle of Cost

There is a golden rule, 'Benefit should be more than the cost'.

Format of a Report

A report may be written in a letter form, a memorandum form or minutes form,

Let us first look at the Letter form.

Address________

Date __________

Address____

Dear Sir(s)______________________________________

Subject ____

____

Para 1____

____

Para 2____

____

Para 3____

____

Para 4____

____

Yours Faithfully,

Sd/-

Designation

Contents [Body of the Report]

Para 1 – Terms of reference

Para 2 – Findings

Para 3 – Observations

Para 4 – Recommendations

The second kind of report is the **Memorandum** form. This is simple and has neither salutation nor complementary close.

This format simplifies and speeds up the communication process.

ABC Automobiles

Delhi

To : ____________________________

From : ______________________

Dated : ______________________

Subject : ______________________

____

____

____

Body of the Report

____

____

____

____

____

____

____

____

The third kind of report is in **Minutes** form.

The minutes form has already been discussed in the chapter on Notice, Agenda and Minutes.

Press Release

Every organization issues press releases to inform the general public about the important events happening within the industry or the organization. Basically, a press release does not bring any monetary gains to either to the organization or the newspapers accepting them or publishing them. The golden rule is, 'Let the world know you exist'.

Hence when, handled properly, the press releases help to publicize a company or an organization and boost its image in the market.

These days a special department called Public Relations Department or the P.R. is created and it has the responsibility of holding press conferences and to issue press releases.

Press releases cover important events like senior appointments, seminars, conferences, visits of VIP's to the organization, introduction of a new product, joint venture, merger and acquisition, etc.

Essential Features of a Good Press Release

Newsworthy

The basic criterion of any press release is that the news should have some value, otherwise no newspaper would publish it.

Factual

An important principle of business communication is integrity.

Organizations need to understand that misrepresentation of facts to reap immediate benefits is bound to backfire.

Conciseness

All along the study of Business Communication, the word conciseness has been talked of quite often. This signifies the importance of being concise. Save time save money. Hence a press release also needs to be brief and to the point, as the whole newspaper will not be given to your press release.

Simplicity

The language used should be simple and easy for the reader to understand.

Suitability

The press release should be published in a suitable newspaper or journal and not just any.

Five Ws

A good press release takes care of five Ws of journalism.

– Who, What, When, Where, Why.

Who? Names of people involved and names can be news worthy.

What?	The press release should be about a news worthy event
When?	The time of the event and time of the press release are important. Old news is no news.
Where?	The venue of the event.
Why?	The event did have a purpose. Mention it.

Apart from the above mentioned essential features, a press release should also

- have a catchy heading,
- be written in third person,
- be written in small paragraphs,
- be edited before passing it on for publishing,
- be interesting, and
- and not sound like an advertisement.

Test Yourself

1. What is the importance of a Report?
2. What are the essential features of a good report?
3. Discuss the Principles of drafting a report.
4. What is a Press release?
5. Discuss the format of a report.
6. What is a press release?
7. Discuss the essential features of a Press release.
8. What are the five Ws?

Chapter 16

E-mail

Learning Objectives

- To get introduced to E-mail
- To understand how to write an E-mail
- To study the E-mail Etiquettes

Introduction to E-Mail

Internet has revolutionized almost all spheres of our life. Even in the field of communication, the use of e-mail has brought about drastic changes.

E-mail has become more popular than any other means of communication. When was the last time you wrote a letter and sent it by post?

Let us look at the reasons of its gaining so much popularity.

- It is a high-speed communication mode.
- It is cheaper and faster than a letter.
- All you need to do is, type your letter on your keyboard and click and send. The transfer of messages is almost instantaneous.
- You can send the same letter, at the same time, to many recipients.
- You can send along any attachment you wish to.
- Time zones do not matter.
- Even faster than a telegram that was used earlier for faster transfer of important messages.
- You may write any length of a letter, it won't cost you more.
- You may receive replies faster as well.
- Hence it is a highly effective, low-cost method of transfer of information.

Writing an E-mail

Since it is a written form of communication, hence all rules of written communication are applicable.

Let us look at the format of the 'box' in which we write an e-mail.

To : Add CC/Add BC
Sub :
Attach a file

'To'

Mention the correct e-mail address of the receiver. You may add more recipients.

'Sub'

This means the subject of your mail. Be crisp and brief and it need not be a complete sentence.

But since this is the first thing that the receiver reads, it should be able to catch his attention.

'Attach file'

Sometimes we wish to send files along the mail and hence may be attached.

The empty box is for your mail on letter.

- It should begin with a 'Greeting' which should spell courtesy.
- A 'Complimentary Close' is also required after the body of the mail.
- The language used should be simple and lucid and again all rules of communication are applicable.
- The paragraphs should be short, crisp and focused.

Generally, abbreviations are not used for business letters (like the ones used to talk to friends.)

However, there are a few abbreviations that are accepted even in the business world.

A few examples are given below:

ASAP	As soon as possible
FYI	For your information
RSVP	Please reply
FAQ	Frequently asked questions
NB	Please note

E-mail Etiquettes

Why does a company need email etiquettes?

It is important for every company to implement etiquette rules for three major reasons:

- **Professionalism**

A proper email language conveys a professional image.

- **Efficiency**

An e-mail that is grammatically correct and has a proper layout is effective than a poorly worded e-mail.

- **Protection from liability**

The awareness of e-mail risks will protect a company from costly law suits.

Let us now look at some E-mail Etiquettes

- **Never make spelling, grammar or punctuation errors**

This is very important as errors in your communication not only give a bad impression of your company, but also hinders the communication process. And, if your program has a spell checking option, why not use it?

- **Let it have a personal touch**

An e-mail should be personally addressed, and should also include a personal i.e. customized content.

- **Answer promptly**

People send an e-mail because they wish to receive a quick response; otherwise they would send a letter or a fax. Therefore, always send across a reply within at least 24 hours, and preferably within the same working day. At least an acknowledgement should be sent across if the reply cannot be sent stating that you will get back to them.

- **Have a good virus scanner in place**

You need to have a good virus scanner in place since your customers will not be very happy if you send them documents full of viruses!

- **A proper structure & layout should be used**

A proper structure and layout gives your content a neat and clean look, and this is appreciated by the receiver.

- **Never write an e-mail in CAPITALS**

IF YOU WRITE IN CAPITALS IT SEEMS AS IF YOU ARE SHOUTING. This can be highly annoying and irritating for the receiver.

- **Reply along with the message thread**

When you reply to an email, you must include the original mail in your reply; hence use the option 'Reply', instead of 'New Mail'. This helps the receiver to save precious time in looking up for the context in which you may have replied.

- **A Company should always add disclaimers to their emails**

It is important for a company to add disclaimers to both internal and external mails, since this can help protect the company from liability.

- **Use abbreviations and emoticons with care**

Generally in business emails, try not to use abbreviations such as BTW (by the way) and LOL (laugh out loud).These are meant to be used b The recipient might not be aware of the meanings of the abbreviations and in business emails these are generally not appropriate.
The same goes for emoticons, such as the smiley :-). If you are not sure whether your recipient knows what it means, it is better not to use it.

- **Give a meaningful subject to your Email**

Always use a subject that is meaningful to the recipient as well as yourself. The subject should also capture the interest of the recipient. For instance, when you send an email to a company requesting information about a product, it is better to mention the actual name of the product, e.g. 'Product A information' than to just say 'product information' or the company's name in the subject.

- **Use active voice instead of passive voice**

The use of active voice adds clarity to our words, whereas the passive voice is more formal and impersonal.

- **Use URGENT and IMPORTANT only for the urgent and important**

Remember always that certain words should only be used when required, don't make a habit of writing urgent or important. Remember the story of the young shepherd who cried 'Wolf, Wolf' just for fun. And one day when the wolf actually came, nobody came to his help.

- **Avoid long sentences**

Try to be as concise as possible. Email is meant to be a quick medium, hence take care not to send emails that are too long.

If a person receives an email that looks like a dissertation, chances are that they will not even attempt to read it!

- **Never send or forward emails containing defamatory, offensive, racist or obscene remarks**

By sending or even just forwarding one offensive remark in an email, you and your company can face court cases resulting in not only penalties but also destroy the image in the market.

- **Never forward virus hoaxes and chain letters**

Beware of virus hoaxes and chain letters as they may contain virus. The best place for them is the Recycle bin.

- **Language gender should be neutral**

Always use words that are free from gender bias. [as discussed in chapter on Principles of Effective Communication]

- **Never reply to spam**

By replying to spam or by unsubscribing, you are confirming that your email address is 'live'. Confirming this will only generate even more spam. Therefore, just hit the delete button or use email software to remove spam automatically.

- **Use cc: field sparingly**

It is advisable to add 'cc' only when this person knows why he is receiving a copy.

Test Yourself

1. Discuss the factors that have made the use of e-mails popular.
2. 'A business e-mail is similar to a business letter'. Comment.
3. What are the essential Email etiquettes used in business?

PART 3

THE BASICS OF GRAMMAR

Chapter 17

Introduction To Grammar

Learning Objectives

- To understand the need of Grammar
- To study the Parts of Speech
- To understand what is :-
  - Noun
  - Pronoun
  - Adjective
  - Verb
  - Adverb
  - Preposition
  - Conjunction
  - Interjection

Why Grammar?

Grammar, according to the Dictionary, means, 'The system of rules implicit in a language, viewed as a mechanism for generating all sentences in that language'.

Therefore, unless we are aware of the various rules to structure our speech or written language, we cannot ever communicate clearly or effectively.

It's not only about English, but it is true for all languages. Without a proper format or structure, communication would be meaningless and the messages or the information conveyed would be unclear.

Therefore, to communicate in a particular language flawlessly, we need to study Grammar, however boring it may sound. It's wrong to assume that, while speaking or writing English or for that matter any language, we need not worry about Grammar.

The truth is, grammatical errors in our oral or written communication hamper the communication process. Also we must remember that English is the de facto language of the internet and the global language of the business world.

Therefore, it is important to have an understanding as to how this language works. And at the end of the day, we would agree that it is worth the effort and the time we put in.

An important fact, we all need to remember is that our technical skills may become obsolete, but our language skills will not. The structure of our language or grammar does not change or changes very slowly.

Also remember that a good portion of your success in any

profession depends not only on your technical skills but also on your basic communication skills. Your ability to communicate effectively and correctly, both orally as well as written, holds the key to your success.

The requirement is not, of course, to make you a grammarian but to make your written and oral communication flawless and effective.

Parts of Speech

In our communication, we use words and traditional grammar classifies words based on eight parts of speech.

1. Noun
2. Pronoun
3. Adjective
4. Verb
5. Adverb
6. Preposition
7. Conjunction
8. Interjection

Each of these explains how a word is used and not what the word is. It happens, often, that a word may be used as a noun in one sentence and a verb in another. Therefore, it is important to understand the correct usage of a word, before we use it.

Let us now understand each of the eight parts of speech.

NOUN

Nouns are words which name a person, place, animal, thing or an abstract idea.

For example: Ganesh, India, Delhi, Lion, Tree, and Wisdom.

An important thing to remember, here, is that a noun can function not only as the subject in a sentence but also as an object, a verb, the object of a preposition, or an appositive.

We can also say in easy words, that whatever exists, we assume, can be named, and that name is a noun.

A Proper Noun is one which names a specific person, place or thing and is always written with a capital letter, whereas, a Common Noun is one which names everything else, things that usually are not written with a capital letter.

For example:

- Proper Noun – Ganesh, India, Ganges.
- Common Noun - Mountain, man, car, country.

Then we have the Abstract Noun that names a quality or concept rather than something concrete.

For example:

Abstract Noun – success, happiness, patience, warmth.

PRONOUN

Pronouns are words that can be used in place of a noun.

Kinds of Pronouns

Personal pronouns are those pronouns that stand for 'three' Persons.

First Person, 'I' and 'We' denote the person or persons speaking.

Second Person, 'You' denotes the person or persons spoken to.

Third Person, 'He, She, It and They' denote the person or persons spoken of.

An important fact to remember is that these pronouns are to be used only as the Subject of a sentence.

When they are to be used as an Object they change accordingly as explained below.

As the SUBJECT	I	We	You	He	She	They	It
As the OBJECT	Me	Us	You	Him	Her	Them	It

Similarly, when personal pronouns are being used to show ownership we call them Possessive Pronouns.

Again they change accordingly as explained below.

As the SUBJECT	I	We	You	He	She	They	It
As the Possessive	My/ Mine	Our/ Ours	Your/ Yours	His/	Her/ Hers	Their/ Theirs	Its

Important Tip

Use my, our, your, her, his, its or their, when the pronoun comes before the noun it modifies.

Use mine, ours your, hers, his or theirs when the pronoun comes after the noun it modifies.

For example:

- This is my book.
- This book is mine.
- This is her house.
- This house is hers.

Important Tip

Do not confuse between possessive pronouns and contractions.

For example:

Its_____ possessive pronoun

It's_____ contraction for 'It is' or 'It has'

- It's time for the mother bird to let go its baby for good.

Important Tip

While using pronouns in Compound subjects and objects, you need to take special care.

For example:

- Raj and I enjoyed the movie. [NOT Raj and me enjoyed the movie.]

- Raj asked Ravi and me for help. [NOT Raj asked Ravi and I for help.]

To avoid making such errors mentally omit the first noun and you will be able to use the correct pronoun.

Important Tip

When the compound objects are preceded by the preposition' between', the pronoun is used as in the object position.

For example:

- Between Raj and me, we could finish the project in time.

[NOT Between Raj and I, we could finish the project in time.]

Important Tip

While comparing, when you use 'than' or 'as' be careful of your selection of the correct pronoun.

For example:

- Ganesh works faster than I.
  [NOT Ganesh works faster than me.]
- Recession affected Ravi more than me.

  [NOT Recession affected Ravi more than I.]

The last of the personal pronouns are the 'Reflexive pronouns'. Remember, always, that a reflexive pronoun cannot be used as the subject of a verb. It can only be used as the object.

SUBJECT Pronoun	I	We	You	He	She	It	They
REFLEXIVE Pronoun	Myself	Ourselves	Yourself	Himself	Herself	Itself	Themself

Let us understand how they form from the Subject Pronoun.

Important Tip

Words like 'ourself, hisself, themself or theirselves' do not exist. Hence, do not use them.

Also, a Reflexive pronoun cannot be ever used unless the noun or pronoun, to which it refers, appears in the same sentence.

For example:

- The house belongs to Sheena and me.
  [NOT The house belongs to Sheena and myself.]
- Sheena finished the entire work herself.

Demonstrative Pronouns are those that are used to point out a thing or things.

Singular	Plural
This	These
That	Those

'This' and 'These' are used to point out things near at hand, whereas, 'That' and 'Those' are used to point things that are remote.

Indefinite Pronouns are pronouns that refer to persons or things in a general way and not in particular.

Singular	Plural
Anyone	Both
Everyone	Few
Each	Many
Either	Others

Adjective

Adjective are words that add something to the meaning of a noun or a pronoun, or we can say they describe or modify nouns or pronouns.

An adjective answers questions about the noun or pronoun they modify or describe, questions such as:

- How many?
- What kind?
- Which one?

The position of the adjective in a particular sentence is usually before the noun or pronoun they are describing, however they may also be placed after the word they describe.

Degrees of Adjectives

Study the following sentences.

- Raj is a good boy.
- Raj is better than Ravi.
- Raj is the best boy in the class.

The words good, better and best are examples of the degrees of adjectives.

The degrees of Comparison as we call them are: Positive, Comparative and the Superlative.

We use the positive degree when there is no comparison being done, the comparative when the comparison is between two things and the superlative when the comparison is among three or more things.

Important Tip

The word 'than' usually accompanies the comparative and the word 'the' always precedes the superlative. The suffixes '-er' and '-est' suffice to form most comparatives and superlatives (rich, richer, richest) although we require '-ier' and '-iest' when a two-syllable word ends in 'y' (funny, funnier, funniest) and otherwise we use 'more' and 'most' when an adjective has more than one syllable (beautiful, more beautiful, most beautiful). However there are certain adjectives which have irregular forms in the comparative and the superlative degrees (good, better, best).

Following is the list of a few Adjectives in the Three Degrees

Rule 1

Positive	**comparative**	**superlative**
Black	blacker	blackest
Bold	bolder	boldest
Bright	brighter	brightest
Brief	briefer	briefest
Calm	calmer	calmest
Clever	cleverer	cleverest
Clean	cleaner	cleanest
Cold	colder	coldest
Deep	deeper	deepest
Dear	dearer	dearest
Gay	Gayer	Gayest
Great	greater	greatest
High	higher	highest
Hard	harder	hardest
Kind	kinder	kindest
Keen	keener	keenest
Light	lighter	lightest
Near	nearer	nearest
Poor	poorer	poorest
Proud	prouder	proudest
Rich	richer	richest
Sweet	sweeter	sweetest
Short	shorter	shortest
Strong	stronger	strongest
Small	smaller	smallest
Tall	taller	tallest
Weak	weaker	weakest
Wild	wilder	wildest
Young	younger	youngest

Rule-2

Positive	**Comparative**	**Superlative**
Able	abler	ablest
Brave	braver	bravest
Fine	finer	finest

Large	larger	largest
Pure	purer	purest
Noble	nobler	noblest
Wise	wiser	wisest
True	truer	truest

Rule- 3

Positive	**Comparative**	**Superlative**
Big	bigger	biggest
Fat	fatter	fattest
Hot	hotter	hottest
Read	reader	reddest
Sad	sadder	saddest
Thin	thinner	thinnest
Wet	wetter	wettest

Rule-4

Positive	**Comparative**	**Superlative**
Dry	drier	driest
Early	earlier	earliest
Easy	easier	easiest
Happy	happier	happiest
Heavy	heavier	heaviest
Healthy	healthier	healthiest
Jolly	foliar	jolliest
Lazy	lazier	laziest
Merry	merrier	merriest
Pretty	prattler	prettiest
Wealthy	wealthier	wealthiest

Rule-5

Positive	**Comparative**	**Superlative**
Active	More active	Most active
Beautiful	More beautiful	Most beautiful
Careful	More careful	Most careful
Cheerful	More cheerful	Most cheerful
Difficult	More difficult	Most difficult
Diligent	More diligent	Most diligent
Harmful	More harmful	Most harmful

Honest	More honest	Most honest
Foolish	More foolish	Most foolish
Important	More important	Most important
Intelligent	More intelligent	Most intelligent
Industrious	More industrious	Most industrious
Interesting	More interesting	most interesting
Obedient	More obedient	Most obedient
Powerful	More powerful	Most powerful
Popular	More popular	Most popular
Urgent	More urgent	Most urgent
Useful	More useful	Most useful

Important Tip

We do not form the comparatives or the superlatives of adjectives which already express an extreme of comparison (chief, absolute, sufficient, impossible, etc).

Whenever there are more than one adjective to be added to a noun or pronoun, we need to remember that there is a specific order of placing them. We usually refer it to as the Royal order of adjectives. It is as follows:

- Determiners (used as an adjective)
- Observation
- Physical Description
    1. Size
    2. Shape
    3. Age
    4. Color
- Origin
- Material
- Qualifier
- Noun

Example

- A beautiful, big old car.

(NOT An old, big, beautiful car)

- Several gorgeous long – stemmed red silk roses.

(NOT Several red long-stemmed silk gorgeous roses)

VERB

A verb is a word that expresses either physical or mental action or a state of being. The verb showing action is called the Main Verb, and the word that expresses the state of being is called the Helping Verb. The verb expresses the time by the form it takes.

There are three forms of verbs:

Present, Past and Past Participle in most cases, the Past Participle forms are formed by adding 'd/ed' to the present form.

However, quite a few verbs form their Past and Past Participle forms in other ways. These are called Irregular verbs.

Following is a list of verbs in the three forms:

GROUP -1

Present (Ist Form)	**Past (2nd Form)**	**Past Participle (3rd Form)**	**Present Participle ing form**
Arise	arose	arisen	arising
Awake	awoke	awoke	awaking
Be	was, were	been	being
Bear	bore	born	bearing
Bear	bore	borne	bearing
Become	became	become	becoming

Begin	began	begun	beginning
Behold	beheld	beheld	beholding
Bend	bent	bent	bending
Bite	bit	bitten	biting
Blow	blew	blown	blowing
Bind	bound	bound	binding
Bid	bade	bidden	bidding
Break	broke	broken	breaking
Choose	chose	chosen	choosing
Cling	clung	clung	clinging
Come	came	come	coming
Dig	dug	dug	digging
Do	did	done	doing
Draw	drew	drawn	drawing
Drink	drank	drunk	drinking
Drive	drove	driven	driving
Eat	ate	eaten	eating
Fall	fell	fallen	falling
Feed	fed	fed	feeding
Find	found	found	finding
Fly	flew	flown	flying
Forbid	forbade	forbidden	forbidding
Forget	forgot	forgotten	forgetting
Freeze	froze	frozen	freezing
Get	got	got	getting

Give	gave	given	giving
Grind	ground	ground	grinding
Hang	hung	hung	hanging
Hide	held	held	holding
Know	knew	known	knowing
Lie	lay	lain	lying
Ride	rode	ridden	riding
Ring	rang	rung	ringing
See	saw	seen	seeing
Shake	shook	shaken	shaking
Shine	shone	shone	shining
Shoot	shot	shot	shooting
Shrink	shrank	shrunk	shrinking
Sing	sang	sung	singing
Sink	sank	sunk	sinking
Sit	sat	sat	sitting
Slay	slew	slain	slaying
Speak	spoke	spoken	speaking
Spit	spat	spat	spitting
Stand	stood	stood	standing
Steal	stole	stolen	stealing
Stick	stuck	stuck	sticking
sting	stung	stung	stinging
Strike	struck	struck	Striking
Swear	swore	sworn	swearing

Swim	swam	swum	swimming
Swing	swung	swung	swinging
Take	took	taken	taking
Tear	tore	torn	tearing
Throw	threw	thrown	throwing
Wear	wore	worn	wearing
Weave	wove	woven	weaving
Win	won	won	winning
Wind	wound	wound	winding
Write	wrote	written	writing
Wring	wrung	wrung	wringing

GROUP II

Present (Ist Form)	Past (2nd Form)	Past Participle (3rd Form)	Present Participle ing form
Abuse	Abused	Abused	Abusing
Act	Acted	Acted	Acting
Add	Added	Added	Adding
Admire	Admired	Admired	Admiring
Advise	Advised	Advised	Advising
Allow	Allowed	Allowed	Allowing
Answer	Answered	Answered	Answering
Appoint	Appointed	Appointed	Appointing
Appear	Appeared	Appeared	Appearing
Arrive	Arrived	Arrived	Arriving

Arrest	Arrested	Arrested	Arresting
Ask	Asked	Asked	Asking
Attack	Attacked	Attacked	Attacking
Bark	Barked	Barked	Barking
Bake	Baked	Baked	Baking
Bathe	Bathed	Bathed	Bathing
Beg	Begged	Begged	Begging
Believe	Believed	Believed	Believing
Behave	Behaved	Behaved	Behaving
Bleed	Bled	Bled	Bleeding
Bless	Blessed	Blessed	Blessing
Break	Broke	Brought	Breaking
Bring	Brought	Brought	Bringing
Boil	Boiled	Boiled	Boiling
Boast	Boasted	Boasted	Boasting
Borrow	Borrowed	Borrowed	Borrowing
Build	Built	Built	Building
Burn	Burnt	Burnt	Burning
Buy	Bought	Bought	Buying
Call	Called	Called	Calling
Carry	Carried	Carried	Carrying
Catch	Caught	Caught	Catching
Clean	Cleaned	Cleaned	Cleaning
Close	Closed	Closed	Closing
Change	Changed	Changed	Changing
Check	Checked	Checked	Checking

Climb	Climbed	Climbed	Climbing
Clap	Clapped	Clapped	Clapping
Copy	copied	copied	Coping
Collect	Copied	Copied	Collecting
Complain	Collected	Collected	Complaining
Complete	Complained	Complained	Completing
Cook	Completed	Completed	Cooking
Count	Cooked	Cooked	Counting
Confuse	Counted	Counted	Confusing
Consult	Confused	Confused	Consulting
Cover	Consulted	Consulted	Covering
Crow	Covered	Covered	Crowing
Cross	Crowed	Crowed	Crossing
Creep	Crept	Crept	Creeping
Cry	Cried	cried	Crying
Decorate	Decorated	Decorated	Decorate
Dance	Danced	Danced	Dancing
Deceive	Deceived	Deceived	Deceiving
Defeat	Defeated	Defeated	Defeating
Decide	Decided	Decided	Deciding
Desire	Desired	Desired	Desired
Discover	Discovered	Discovered	Discovering
Dip	Dipped	Dipped	Dipping
Die	Died	Died	Dying
Divide	Divided	Divided	Dividing
Dream	Dreamt	Dreamt	Dreaming

Dry	Dried	Dried	Drying
Drown	Drowned	Drowned	Drowning
Dye	Dyed	Dyed	Dyeing
Earn	Earned	Earned	Earning
Enter	Entered	Entered	Entering
Employ	Employed	Employed	Employing
Explain	Explained	Explained	Explaining
Examine	Examined	Examined	Examining
Face	faced	faced	facing
Fail	failed	failed	falling
Fear	feared	feared	fearing
Feed	Fed	fed	feeding
Feel	felt	felt	feeling
Fell	felled	felled	felling
Flee	fled	fled	fleeing
Fight	fought	fought	fighting
Finish	finished	finished	finishing
Fine	fined	fined	fining
Float	floated	floated	floating
Graze	grazed	grazed	grazing
Gather	gathered	gathered	gathering
Have	had	had	having
Hate	hated	hated	hating
Hang	hanged	hanged	hanging
Hear	heard	heard	hearing
Help	helped	helped	helping

Improve	improved	improved	improving
Invite	invited	invited	inviting
Join	joined	joined	joining
Jump	jumped	jumped	jumping
Keep	kept	kept	keeping
Kill	killed	killed	killing
Knit	knitted	knitted	knitting
kneel	knelt	knelt	kneeling
lay	laid	laid	laying
lie	licd	lied	lying
laugh	laughed	laughed	laughing
learn	learnt	learnt	learning
leave	left	left	leaving
lend	lent	lent	lending
lose	lost	lost	losing
like	liked	liked	liking
Listen	listened	listened	listening
look	looked	looked	looking
live	lived	lived	living
love	loved	loved	loving
lead	led	lcd	leading
Marry	married	married	marrying
make	made	made	making
mcan	meant	meant	meaning
meet	met	met	meeting
move	moved	moved	moving

melt	melted	melted	melting
mend	mended	mended	mending
mix	mixed	mixed	mixing
name	named	named	naming
need	needed	needed	needing
Nip	nipped	nipped	nipping
Obey	obeyed	obeyed	obeying
Open	opened	opened	opening
Order	ordered	ordered	ordering
Oppose	opposed	opposed	opposing
pay	paid	paid	paying
play	played	played	playing
pray	prayed	prayed	praying
praise	praised	praised	praising
preach	preached	preached	preaching
Peep	Peeped	Peeped	Peeping
plant	planted	planted	planting
pluck	plucked	plucked	plucking
prepare	prepared	prepared	preparing
pull	pulled	pulled	pulling
prevent	prevented	prevented	preventing
Punish	punished	punished	punishing
Prove	proved	proved	proving
Promise	promised	promised	promising
Push	pushed	pushed	pushing
plough	ploughed	ploughed	ploughing

Quarrel	quarrelled	quarrelled	quarrelling
rain	rained	rained	raining
Reply	replied	replied	replying
reach	reached	reached	reaching
receive	received	received	receiving
refuse	refused	refused	refusing
rest	rested	rested	resting
resign	resigned	resigned	resigning
repair	repaired	repaired	repairing
Remember	remembered	remembered	remembering
return	returned	returned	returning
Roar	roared	roared	roaring
say	said	said	saying
seek	sought	sought	seeking
sell	sold	sold	selling
save	saved	saved	saving
saw	sawed	sawed	sawing
send	sent	sent	sending
select	selected	selected	selecting
sleep	slept	slept	sleeping
stand	stood	stood	standing
stay	stayed	stayed	staying
spend	spent	spent	spending
Stop	stopped	stopped	stopping
sweep	swept	swept	sweeping
study	studied	studied	stuying

slip	slipped	slipped	slipping
talk	talked	talked	talking
tell	told	told	telling
teach	taught	taught	teaching
think	thought	thought	thinking
Tie	tied	tied	tying
touch	touched	touched	touching
try	tried	tried	trying
trust	trusted	trusted	trusting
use	used	used	using
understand	understood	understood	understanding
walk	walked	walked	walking
wash	washed	washed	washing
wait	waited	waited	waiting
weep	wept	wept	weeping
work	worked	worked	working
watch	watched	watched	watching
wish	wished	wished	wishing
wander	wandered	wandered	wandering
waste	wasted	wasted	wasting
wed	wedded	wedded	wedding
wound	wounded	wounded	wounding
worship	worshipped	worshipped	worshipping
wonder	wondered	wondered	wondering
wrap	wrapped	wrapped	wrapping
yield	yielded	yielded	yielding

GROUP –III

Present (Ist Form)	Past (2nd Form)	Past Participle (3rd Form)	Present Participle ing form
Bid	Bid	Bid	Biding
Bet	Bet	Bet	Betting
Burst	Burst	Burst	Bursting
Cast	Cast	Cast	Casting
Cost	Cost	Cost	Costing
Cut	Cut	Cut	Cutting
Hurt	Hurt	Hurt	Hurting
Let	Let	Let	Letting
Put	Put	Put	Putting
Read	Read	Read	Reading
Set	Set	Set	Setting
Shed	Shed	Shed	Shedding
Shut	Shut	Shut	Shutting
Spread	Spread	Spread	Spreading
Thrust	Thrust	Thrust	Thrusting
Quit	Quit	Quit	Quitting

ADVERB

Adverbs are words that add something to the meaning of a verb, another adverb or an adjective. Consider the following examples:

- John walks (verb) slowly (adverb).
- John walks very (adverb) slowly (adverb).
- Taj is a very beautiful (adverb) building (adjective).

Many adverbs are made by adding '-ly' to the end of adjectives.

For example:

Slow ~~~~~~~~ Slowly

Careful ~~~~~~~~ Carefully

However, lots of adverbs are irregular.

The placement of an adverb in a sentence is also very important, because placing the same sentence at different meaning.

Consider the following examples.

- Only he gave me notes. (Meaning no one else gave me notes)
- He only gave me notes. (Meaning he did not give notes to anyone else)
- He gave me only notes. (Meaning he did not give me anything else but notes)

PREPOSITION

A preposition is a word which shows the relationship between noun or a pronoun and some other word in the sentence.

For example:

The cat is on the mat.

He left his home at midnight.

They arrived in India on Monday.

Let us understand how and when a Preposition may be used:

	AT	IN	ON
1.	'At' usually denotes a definite point of time but can also be used for indefinite periods.	'In' used with parts of the day, month, year, season.	'On' is used with days dates, and day + morning, evening.

	E.g.: At 3:30a.m., at midnight, at dawn, at night, at Christmas, at Diwali.	E.g. In the morning, in summer, in March, In 2004.	E.g. On Monday, on 5th May, on the Dial day, On Christmas eve, On Sunday afteınoon.
2.	'At' has the idea of an exact point; it is used with villages, small towns, places of residence, streets E. g. at C. P., at Ambala, at Victoria street, at H. No. 40, at sector-50	It has the idea of larger area and is used while speaking of bigger towns, states, countries. E. g. In India, in New Delhi, in the middle, in a bank.	On is used in speaking of things at rest (surface –to- surface contact). E. g. on the table, on the soft, on the chair.
3.	At conveys the idea of general neighborhood. E.g. on a piece of E. g. in the drawer, E.g. at the table, at the next Crossing.	In conveys the idea of something contained. paper, in the closet.	On conveys the idea of resting on something. on the internet.
4.	At has the idea of hitting. E.g. She threw the stone at the dog.	In suggests the interior of anything E. g. Today she is in a bad mood.	On suggests the idea of resting on something. E.g. I depend on my parents' help.

FROM:

It is used with:

- The point of departure

For example

- She had left from the office.
- To express the source of something

For example

- I have received a gift from my father.

- Before the starting time of an action. It is followed by to / till.

For example My exam is from 8.00 am to 11.00a.m.

Off: shows separation. It is red in the sense of from the source of down from.

For example

- The book fell off the table.
- Switch off the light.

ROUND: it used for circular motion.

For example

The dog went round the tree.

ACROSS: means on the other side.

For example

The D.P.S. is across the road.

UPON: as used to denote motion.

For example

The cat sprang upon the table.

DURING: It is used to express an idea:

(a) That an action persists throughout the whole of specified period.

For example

During the war the food was rationed.

(b) That an event took place or is to take place at any time within a specified period of time.

For example

The theft took place during the night.

OUT OF: It is the opposite of 'into' it means 'from the interior of

For example

The bird flew out of the cage.

BY /WITH:

By is used with the doer of an action.

With is used with the object with which the action is done.

For example

The old man was beaten by the stranger with a stick.

BESIDES: Means in addition to

For example

Besides Hindi and English, I know French.

ON TIME: Means at the exact time, not before, not after.

For example

He reached the station in time for the train.

AFTER: After is used to denote some period of time in the past.

For example

She came back after an hour.

IN: is used to denote some period of time in the future.

For example

She will come back in an hour.

WITHIN: means before the end of

For example

I shall be back within a week.

OF: 1. it suggests belonging.

For example

One leg of this chair is broken.

2. It means pertaining to.

For example

She often talks of you.

ABOUT: it suggests the subject of book, conversation.

For example

He told us about his trip to Goa.

PAST:

She walked past me without greeting me.

BY: Is used for means of transport.

For example

He went to office by car.

Special phrases in which prepositions are used:

At:

at home. at school, at work, at first, at last, at rest, at a loss, at all costs, at all at once .

BY:

By chance, by Heart, by Mistake, by Day (night), by the way,

one by one, step by step.

FOR:

For example, Forever, for good, for the first time, for the moment,

for the time being

FROM:

From bad to worse, from day to day, from memory, from Morning till night.

ON:

On behalf of, on the contrary, on foot, on sale,on the whole

UNDER:

Under discussion, under the circumstances, under the impression,

Under treatment, under repair, under the rules, under control.

IN :

In love with, in need of, in fact in general, in the meantime,

in the long run, in one' s opinion, in (under)these cicumstances.

CONJUNCTION

A conjunction is a word that joins two words, two groups of words or two sentences.

For example:

Raja and Ravi went to the market.

It was raining so did not go to the market.

INTERJECTION

An interjection is a word that expresses strong or sudden emotions. Interjections are more often used in spoken langrage than in written language.

For example;

Hurrah! India has won the match.

Wow! That is a beautiful dress.

Chapter 18

Subject-Verb Agreement

Learning Objectives

- To understand the concept of Subject-Verb Agreement
- To study the rules of Subject-Verb Agreement

Introduction

The subject-verb agreement is one of the main portions of grammar where you would find, majority of the people making mistakes.

The basic rule of subject-verb agreement is that a verb must agree with its subject in number and person.

If the subject in sentence is singular, it takes a singular verb. If the subject is plural, it takes a plural verb.

It is very commonly observed that in identifying whether a subject is singular or plural people make mistakes. Hence to make the subject and verb agree, you must first be able to identify both.

In many sentences, identifying a subject is easy. Let us consider the following examples.

- A manager needs to motivate his subordinates.
- The children play in this garden every evening.

In the first sentence the subject is 'a manager' which is single, hence takes a singular verb, where as the subject 'the children' in the next sentence is plural, hence takes a plural verb.

However, in some sentences, identifying is not so easy. Let us consider the following examples.

- Every rule and regulation is (not 'are') to be reviewed.

In this sentence the verb needs to agree with 'every' which is singular.

RULES

Rule 1:

Sometimes the subject is separated from its verb by a phrase or a clause.

In such cases care should be taken in identifying the subject.

For example:

- All the students of this college have left for the day.
- The cost of all essential commodities has gone up.

In the first sentence the subject is 'All the students' which is plural hence it takes the plural verb 'have'

However in the second sentence the subject is the cost and hence even if the word 'all ' is there the verb used is singular.

Rule 2:

When a sentence begins with 'there' the verb must agree with the subject that follows it.

For example:

- There are many apples in the fridge.
- There is a bird sitting on the tree.

Rule 3:

A plural verb is used, when two or more singular nouns or pronouns are joined by 'and'

For example:

- An apple and a banana are kept on the table.
- My friend and her sister are coming to my home today.

Exception:

There are some exceptions to this Rule.

- If two nouns joined by 'and' refer to the same person or thing, singular verb is used.

For example:

- The poet and philosopher is dead.
- The poet and the philosopher are dead.

Compare the above two examples. In the first sentence the poet and philosopher refers to one person as there is no determiner before the second noun.

However in the second sentence the poet and the philosopher refer to two different persons, therefore; we use a singular verb in the first case and a plural verb in the second.

- If two nouns, although joined by 'and' but express a single idea, a singular verb is used.

For example:

- Time and tide waits for none.
- All work, and no play makes Jack a dull boy.

- If two nouns having similar meaning 'and' are placed together for emphasis, a singular verb is used.

For example:

- Power and position holds no charm for him.
- Slow and steady wins the race.

Rule 4:

Certain indefinite pronouns are treated as singular hence, carry a singular verb.

For example:

- Each of the boys is going to Mumbai.
- Either of you is suitable for the post.
- None of these bags is mine.
- Neither of these boys is suitable for the post.

Rule 5:

When two nouns or pronouns are connected by 'either....... or', 'neither............ nor' or 'not only............but also' the verb must agree with the latter noun or pronoun.

For example:

- Either she or her friends are or her friends are to blame.
- Neither her friends nor she is to blame.

Rule 6:

When two nouns or pronouns are connected with 'as well as', 'with', 'together with', etc, the verb must agree with the first subject.

For example:

- The teacher as well as the students is absent.
- The students as well as the teacher are absent.

Rule 7:

Some nouns which are although, plural in form but singular in meaning take a singular verb, for example:

- Twenty miles is a long distance to travel on foot.
- Politics is a dirty game.

Rule 8:

Then there are nouns which are singular in form but plural in meaning, hence they take a plural verb.

For example:

- The cattle are grazing in the valley.
- The people are enjoying the weather.

Rule 9:

Collective nouns such as army, police, jury, parliament etc, take a singular verb when considered as a whole and take a plural verb when we talk of its members individually.

For example:

- The jury has given the decision.
- The jury are divided on this issue.

Rule 10:

A pair of jeans, a pair of shoes, etc. are treated as singular hence take a single verb.

A lot of, some of, most of, a great deal of, etc take a singular verb when they refer to amount whereas they take a plural verb when they refer to number.

For example:

- Some of the students were absent.
- A pair of shoes is all that I wish to buy today.
- Italian leather shoes are quite expensive.
- Some of the work is still left undone.

Rule 11:

Whenever the subject is a relative pronoun, the verb agrees with the antecedent of the relative pronoun

For example:

- God helps those who help themselves.
- She is one of the best mothers that have ever lived.

Test Yourself

Circle the correct word

1. He and I.................. (Am, is, are,) great friends.
2. Slow and steady .... (Went, wins) the race.
3. Early to bed and early to rise................. (Made, modes) man healthy, wealthy and wise.
4. The orator and the statesman............ (Has, have) arrived.
5. Every Man and woman in the village............ (Was, were) terrified.
6. Either Mohan or Sohan .... (is, are) in the wrong bus.
7. Neither Mohan nor his friends.............. (Was, were) present.
8. Either you or he .... (As, am, are) telling a lie.
9. Raman, as well as his friends, (as, am, are) going for the trip.
10. The king and all his ministers, (was, were) killed.

Chapter 19

Articles

Learning Objectives

- To study about Definite & Indefinite Articles
- To know the Correct Usage of Articles
- To understand the Omission of Articles

Definite & Indefinite Articles

There are three articles: a, an, the.

'A' and 'an' are called indefinite articles as these do not refer or point to a particular person or thing.

'A' and 'an' can be used with countable singular nouns.

'The' is a definite article and it can replace 'a' or 'an' when referring to a particular person or thing.

'The' can be used for countable as well as uncountable and singular as well as plural nouns.

Correct Usage

Indefinite Articles

The usage of 'a or an' depends on the beginning sound of the noun.

There are two divisions of the English alphabet.

Vowels:

'a, e, i, o, u'

Consonants:

All alphabets, except the vowels.

We use 'an' before all words that begin not with the vowel, but with the vowel sound.

For example:

- An umbrella
- A university

Although, the above nouns, 'umbrella and university' begin with **'u'** however **'an'** is still not used in both cases.

This is because university begins with a consonant sound of 'Yu'.

Therefore, it is important to know the correct pronunciation of word to be able to add an article correctly.

Usage of 'A'

- With a singular countable noun beginning with a consonant and consonant sound.

For example:

A cat

A house

A book

A teacher

- With a singular countable noun beginning with the vowel E or U but having a consonant sound of 'yu'

For example:

A uniform

A European

A university

- With singular countable noun beginning with the vowel O but having a consonant sound of 'wa'

For example:

A one – rupee coin

A one – eyed man

Usage of 'An'

- With a singular countable noun beginning with a vowel and having a vowel sound.

For example:

An orange

An umbrella

An egg

An inkpot

- With a singular countable noun beginning with a consonant yet having a vowel sound.

Especially in the case of abbreviations.

For example:

An M.P.

An MLA

- With a singular countable noun beginning with the consonant 'h' that is but silent.

For example:

An hour

An heir

An honest girl

Definite Article

The definite article 'the' is used in the following cases:

- When we are talking of a particular person or thing.

For example:

The man standing outside has come for the interview.

- When a singular noun represents an entire species.

For example:

The rose is a beautiful flower.

We add 'the' before the names of :

- Unique objects

the sun, the moon, the earth.

- Directions

The north, the east

- Rivers, Oceans, lakes

The Ganges, the Indian ocean, the Dal Lake

- Mountain Ranges

The Himalayas, the Deccan Plateau

- Desserts

The Thar Desert, the Sahara Desert

- Newspapers, magazines

The Times of India, the Hindu

- Holy Books

The Gita , the Quran, the Guru Granth Sahib, the Bible

- Trains, Ships Airways

The Shatabdi the Vikrant, the Indian Airways

- Important buildings

The Parliament House, the Rashtrapati Bhawan

- Countries & provinces with descriptive name

The USA, the UK

- Before an adjective in its superlative form

The best, the most beautiful

- Before ordinal numbers

The first, the second

- Before the date

The 15th of August

- Before a proper noun being used as a common noun.

  Kalidas is the Shakespeare of India.

- Before an adjective in a comparative degree if not followed by than

  She is the better of the two friends.

- Before an abstract noun being used in a particular sense

  Everyone praised the wisdom of the young boy.

- Natives of nation

  The Indian people

Omission of Articles

The article is omitted before the following:

- Proper nouns:

Delhi, Govind

- Abstract nouns:

Honesty, wisdom

- Languages

Hindi, English

[The Chinese speak Chinese.]

Note the usage and omission of 'the'. When we say 'the Chinese' we are talking of the natives of China, however we omit 'the' before the next Chinese because here we are referring to the language.

- Before the names of the mountains.

  Mount Everest, Nanda Devi

Test Yourself

Fill in the blanks with a, an the or $

1. I found................bag on...............road...............bag contained................book, ... Calculator and ....pen and ....one rupee coin.

2. ....apple ....day keeps ....doctor away.

3. I bought ....hen , ...horse and ....elephant............ hen lid......................egg but ....house stopped over it .... elephant got angry and kicked ....horse.

Chapter 20

Tenses

Learning Objectives

- To understand the Present, Past & Future Tenses

TENSES

People understand 'Tense" as time, but these must not be confused.

The word 'tense' stands for Present (V1), Past (V2) and Past Participle (V3) forms of verbs.

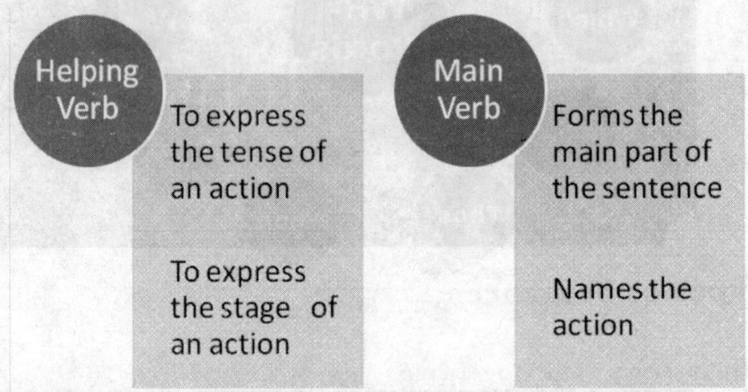

Fig. 20.1

Tenses

Verb Tense Overview with Examples

Simples Present	Simple Past	Simple Future
I study English every day.	Two years ago, I studied English.	If you are having problems, I will you study English. I am going to study English next year.

Present Continuous	Past Continuous	Future Continuous
I am studying English now	I was studying English when you called yesterday.	I will be studying English when you arrive tonight.
I have studied English in several different countries.	I had studied a little English before I moved to Delhi.	I will have studied every tense by the time I finish this course.
I have been studying English for five years.	I had been studying English for five years before I moved to Delhi.	I will have been studying English for over two hours by the time you arrive.

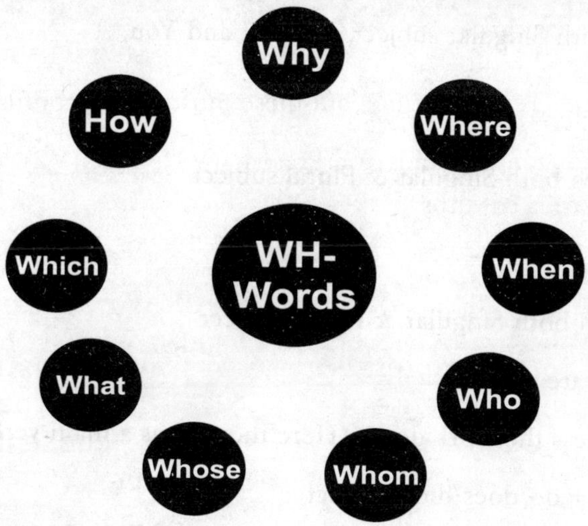

Fig. 20.2

Verb Tense

Types of Sentences

Affirmative :- Subject + Helping Verb + Main Verb + Object

e.g.:- I am reading a book.

Negative :- 'not' :- subject + Helping Verb + Not + Main Verb + Object

e.g.:- I am not reading a book.

Interrogative :- Helping Verb +not + Main Verb + Object?

e.g. Am I not reading a book?

Double Interrogative :- Wh-word + Helping Verb + Sub + (not) + Main Verb + Object?

e.g. :- When will you be washing these clothes?

NOTE: - Question and answer should have the same tense i.e. the helping verb should be the same in both of them.

e.g. :- They are reading a book.

Q. Are they reading a book?

Correct Usage of 'Do/Does/Did'

Present Tense

Do: Is used with Plural subject, I, & you

Does: Is used with Singular subject, except I and You

Past Tense

Did: Is used with both Singular & Plural subject

Future Tense

Do: Is used with both Singular & Plural subject

Their functions are:

- To express the work done: (Here they act as a main verb).

  Subject + do/does/did + object

  e.g.:- 1. I do my home work regularly.

  2. She does her exercises regularly.

  3. He did learn his lessons.

- To emphasize: (Here they act as a helping verb)

  Subject + do/ does/ did +main verb +object

Important Tip

The Verb is Always in the First Form when the helping verb is do/ does/ did.

PRESENT TENSE

SIMPLE PRESENT :-

It is used to express what is actually happening at the present moment; custom or habit or a universal truth (General fact) or daily routine.

Affirmative: Singular sub + V1 + s/es + Object

Plural sub. (we, they), I, you + V1 + object.

- She goes for a walk every morning.
- They go for a walk every morning.

Negative: Subject +Do / Does + not + V1 + Object

- He does not go for a walk every morning.

Interrogative: Do/ Does + Sub. + not + V1 Object?

Do – used with plural sub., I & U

Does – used with Singular Subject.

- Does he go for a walk every morning?
- Do they go for a walk every morning?

SIMPLE PAST:

It is used to express an action that took place in the past time.

Affirmative:

Subject + V2 +Object + TOP (Time of past)

- She went for a walk in the morning.

Negative:

Subject + did + not + V1 + Object + TOP

- She did not go for a walk in the morning.

Interrogative:

Did + Subject + (not) + V1 + Object + TOP?

- Did she not go for a walk in the morning?

Daily Routine in the past :

Subject + used to + V1 + Object + TOP

- He used to go to school on foot.

SIMPLE FUTURE:

It is used to express an action or event that will take place in the future.

Affirmative:

Sub + Will/shall + V1 + object + TOF (Time of future).

- She will go for a walk in the morning.

Will: is used with he, she, you, it, they

Shall: is used with I, we.

Negative:

Subject + will/shall + not+V1 Object + TOF

- She will not go for a walk in the morning.

Interrogative:

Will/shall + subject + not + V1 Object + TOF?

- Will she go for a walk in the morning?

All Time Action:

It is used to express an action that happens all the time round the clock or is a universal truth.

It is expressed using the word 'always' except for universal truth.

PRESENT :- Subject + always + V1 + s/es + Object

- She always goes for a walk in the morning.

PAST :- Subject + always + used to + object + TOP

- She always used to go for a walk in the morning.

FUTURE :- Subject + will/shall + always + be + V1 + ing + object+TOF

She will always go for a walk in the morning.

CONTINUOUS TENSE

PRESENT CONTINUOUS

It is used to express an action that is going on at the time of speaking.

Affirmative:

Subject + is/am/are + V1 + ing + Object

Is : is used with singular object

Am :- is Used with 'I'

Are:- Is used with plural subject, you

- She is reading a book.
- We are reading a book.

Negative:

Subject + is/am/are + not + V1 + ing + object

- I am not reading a book.
- We are not reading books.

Interrogative:

1. Am I reading a book?
2. Are we not reading a book?

PAST CONTINUOUS

It is used to express an action that began and was continuing in the past when another action took place.

Affirmative:

Subject + was /were +V1 + ing + object + 2ndAction+TOP

2nd Action = subject + V2

- She was reading a book when I called her up in the morning.

Negative:

Subject +was/were + not+V1 + ing + Object + 2nd action+ TOP

- She was not reading a book when I called her up in the afternoon.

Interrogative:

Was/were + Subject + (not) + V1 + ing + Object + 2nd Action+ TOP

- Was she not reading a book when I called her up in the afternoon?

FUTURE CONTINUOUS

It is used to express an action that will begin and will be continuing in the future when another action takes place.

Affirmative:

Subject + will/shall + be + V1 + ing + object+ 2nd Action + TOF

2nd Action = subject + V1

e.g. :- She will be reading a book when I call her up in a little while.

Negative:

Subject + will/shall + not + be+ V1 + ing + object +2nd Action + TOF

- She will not be reading a book when I call her up in a little while.

Interrogative:

Will/shall + subject + (not) + be + V1 + ing + object +2nd Action + TOF

- Will she (not) be reading a book in the afternoon?

Intention to Do an Action

It is expressed using the 'going to' form.

GOING TO :

1. We use the 'going to' form to suggest people's intention to do something in the near future.

- We are going to shift to a new house tomorrow.

2. We use this form to make predictions about the future when there are clear signs that this prediction will come true.

- Look at the careless manner in which he is playing. He is going to get out soon.

WILL/SHALL OR GOING TO :

1. We use 'will/shall' to talk about things in the future, which we cannot control, which are decided while speaking.

- We will shift to a house if the landlord increases the rent. (We are deciding it)

2. We use 'going to' form to talk about intentions, about things we have already decided to do.

- The landlord is increasing the rent. We are going to shift a new house. (We have already decided to do so)

PRESENT PERFECT

1. It is used to express an action that began in the past and continued up to the present moment.
2. A completed action, which is connected through its result with the present moment.
3. The experience, which the speaker or a writer has had.
4. An action that recently finished or feeling of present is there.

Affirmative:

Subject + Has/Have+V3 +Object

Has:-is used with singular subject

Have: - is used with plural sub., I & you.

- She has eaten her food.
- I have eaten my food.
- He has eaten his food.

Negative :-

Subject + has/have + not + V3 + object

- She has not eaten her food.

Interrogative :-

Has/Have + subject + V3 + object?

- Has she eaten her food?

PAST PERFECT

It is used to express an action that completed in the past before another action took place.

Affirmative:

Subject + had + V3 + Object + 2nd Action + TOP

Adverbs of time: (Before, After, When)

- The train had left before I reached the station in the afternoon.
- The train had (already) left when I reached the station in the afternoon.
- The train had left after I reached the station in the afternoon.
- She had done her work yesterday.

Negative:

Subject + Has/Have + not + V3 + object +2nd Action + TOP

- She had not done her work yesterday.

Interrogative:

Had + subject + V3 + object + subject + V2 +TOP +?

e.g. :- Had she done her work yesterday?

FUTURE PERFECT

It is used to express an action that will be completed in the future when another action takes place.

Affirmative:

Subject + will/shall + have+ V3 + Object+2nd Action+ TOF

- The train will have left before I reach the station in little while. or
- When I reach the station in a little while, the train will have (already) left.
- I shall have done my work by 6 p.m.

Negative:

Subject +will/shall + have + not + V3 + object + TOF

- I shall have not done my work by 6 p.m.

Interrogative:

Will/shall + subject + have + V3 + object + subject + V1 + TOF +?

- Will you have done your work by 6 p.m.?

Important Tip

Time Period is always added in a sentence in Perfect Continuous Tense.

Also remember that Time Period is mentioned before the Time of the action.

PRESENT PERFECT CONTINUOUS

This is an action that began in the past and is continuing in the present for sometime.

Affirmative:

Subject + has/have + been + V1 + object + + time period

Since – is used for point of time. (Watch or Calendar, Day, Date, Month, Year).

For – is used for period of time (calculated).

- She has been sleeping since morning.

- They have been living in Delhi for 5 years [OR since 2005].

Negative:

Subject + has/have + not been + V1 + ing + object + time period.

- She has not been sleeping since morning.

Interrogative:

Has/ have + Sub + (not) + been + V1 + ing + Object + Time Period +?

- Has she not been sleeping since morning?

PAST PERFECT CONTINUOUS

This is an action that began in the past and was continuing for sometime when another action took place.

Affirmative:

Subject + had been + V1 + ing + object + time period+ 2nd Action + TOP

- She had been ironing the clothes for two hours when the light went off at 4.00 p.m.
- Children had been playing in the garden all day on Sunday.

Negative:

Subject + had +not been + V1 + ing + Object + Time Period + Subject + V2 + TOP

e.g. :- Children had not been playing in the garden all day on Sunday.

Interrogative:

Had + Subject + (not) + been + V1 + ing + Object + Time Period + subject + V2 + TOP

e.g. :- Had children been playing in the garden all day on Sunday.

FUTURE PERFECT CONTINUOUS

This is an action that will begin in the future and will be continuing for sometime when another action takes place.

Affirmative:

Subject + will/ shall + have been + V1 +ing + object + time period + 2nd Action+ TOF

- I shall have been living in Delhi for 15 year in 2006.
- He will have been working in this Institute for three years in June.
- They will have been learning their lessons for 1 hour when their mother reaches home at 5.00 p.m.

Negative:

Subject + will/ shall + have + not + been + V1 + ing + Object + time Period + 2nd Action+ TOF

- He will not have been working in this Institute for three years in June.

Interrogative:

Will/ shall + subject + (not) + been + V1 ing +Object + time Period + 2nd Action+ TOF

- Will he not have been working in this Institute for three years in June?

Forced/Pre-Planned Action

It is used to express:

- Commitment
- External pressure
- Circumstances
- Pre-planning

PRESENT:-

Subject + has/ have to + V1 + object + Reason[Any form of present tense]

- I have to clean my room today as my mother has asked me to do so.
- She has to go to the doctor today as she is not feeling well.

PAST:-

Subject + had to + V1 + object + Reason [Any form of past tense]

- I had to clean my room today as my mother had asked me to do so.
- She had to go to the doctor today as she was not feeling well.

FUTURE:-

Subject + will/ shall + have to + V1 + object + Reason [Any form of present or future tense]

- I shall have to clean my room today otherwise my mother will scold me.
- She will have to go to the doctor today as she is not feeling well.

Test Yourself

1. What is the Present, Past & Future Tenses?

Chapter 21

Vocabulary Building

Learning Objectives

- To study the common Colloquial Phrases
- To learn some Synonyms
- To learn some Antonyms
- To understand the Words Often Confused
- To learn the common One Word Substitution

COLLOQUIAL PHRASES

BREAK

Break away	- escape
Break down	- fail to act
Break into	- enter by force
Break off	- put an end
Break out	- suddenly begin
Break down	- lose control

CALL

Call at	- make a short visit
Call for	- demand
Call in	- ask to come summon
Call off	- stop
Call on	- visit
Call out	- shout
Call up	- telephone

BRING

Bring about	- cause to happen
Bring in	- to import/produce
Bring up	- look after during childhood
Bring around	- to convince

CARRY

Carry away	- remove

Carry away	- excited by unreasonable emotions
Carry on	- continue
Carry out	- fulfill, perform
Carry off	- to handle with success
Carry through	- to get done accomplish

COME

Come about	- happen
Come across	- meet by chance
Come back	- return
Come into	- enter
Come into	- to get, acquire
Come into	- use, be used
Come on	- hurry up
Come along	- make haste
Come up	- make progress
Come up	- ascend
Come up	- was mentioned

LOOK

Look after	- take care of
Look into	- examine, go
Look for	- try to find
Look forward to	- expect
Look out	- be careful
Look out	- watch for
Look up	- (a friend) goes & sees or pays a visit

Look up (a work)	- search for it in a dictionary
Look upon or on	- consider regard

MAKE

Make for	- go towards
Make fun of	- laugh at
Make haste	- hurry up/hasten
Make out	- see, hear or understand
Made up	- invent/compose
Make up for	- compensate
Make up of	- is (or are) composed of
Make up one's mind	- decide/determine
Make do	- to get along or manage with what is available

PUT

Put back	- replace
Put forward	- suggest
Put into	- translate
Put off	- postpone

SYNONYMS

Word	Synonym	Synonym
abandon	discard	vacate
accord	agree	grant
adversity	difficulty	misfortune
affluent	plentiful	rich

aggravate	annoy	infuriate
alleviate	lighten	mitigate
amenable	agreeable	favorable
anguish	distress	sorrow
apathetic	dispirited	lifeless
arrogant	disdainful	imperious
astonish	confound	overwhelm
atrocious	appalling	detestable
augment	add	enlarge
avoid	ignore	shun
awkward	graceless	inept
baffle	confuse	deceive
banal	common	plain
barren	desolate	sterile
berate	criticize	disapprove
betray	deceive	fool
bias	inclination	predisposition
bitter	acrid	sour
blend	combine	mix
bliss	happiness	joy
bluff	boast	feign
bold	daring	fearless
bonus	award	gift
bother	annoy	irritate
brief	concise	short
brilliant	clever	intelligent

brisk	fast	swift
budget	allot	plan
candid	honest	truthful
caricature	cartoon	imitation
casual	informal	natural
category	classification	division
cease	desist	stop
chaotic	disordered	messy
cherish	esteem	love
circumvent	avoid	go around
commemorate	celebrate	honor
compensate	balance	recompense
competent	able	capable
conceive	design	plan
confirmation	acknowledgement	proof
contradict	deny	oppose
contribution	donation	grant
courteous	polite	wellmannered
craving	desire	longing
credulous	confident	trustful
damp	moist	wet
dare	challenge	defy
decay	decline	rot
decent	honorable	pure
dense	filled	packed
designate	name	select

detain	hold	keep
disclose	announce	reveal
dogma	belief	view
durable	constant	lasting
dwindle	abate	diminish
eager	earnest	keen
eccentric	abnormal	idiosyncratic
elaborate	embellish	enhance
emanate	arise	radiate
embezzle	purloin	steal
eminent	distinguished	prominent
encourage	foster	induce
endure	last	persist
essential	cultured	learned
essential	basic	necessary
estimate	guess	predict
evaluate	appraise	judge
exhaust	deplete	empty
exhilarated	cheerful	zestful
explicit	definite	specific
fastidious	exacting	particular
federation	alliance	band
feeble	helpless	infirm
fervor	intensity	passion
feud	argument	dispute
filth	dirt	squalor

flatter	compliment	praise
fleet	nimble	swift
frivolous	inconsequential	trivial
frugal	prudent	saving
furious	angry	outraged
generous	benevolent	unselfish
genuine	actual	real
glare	gleam	glisten
gloomy	cheerless	dim
goad	provoke	badger
grasp	grab	hold
greed	avarice	longing
guarantee	assure	pledge
guile	cunning	deceit
gullible	credulous	unsuspicious
habitual	accustomed	regular
handicap	disability	disadvantage
harass	annoy	disturb
harmless	innocuous	inoffensive
harsh	hard	coarse
hasty	abrupt	hurried
haughty	arrogant	pretentious
humiliate	humble	shame
hygiene	cleanliness	sanitation
hypocrisy	duplicity	falseness
ideal	goal	perfection

idle	lazy	unoccupied
ignorant	stupid	unintelligent
illogical	incongruent	rambling
illustrious	eminent	famous
imitate	copy	reflect
immense	huge	mammoth
impartial	candid	impersonal
impatient	anxious	eager
implicate	accuse	insinuate
importune	beg	solicit
inadvertent	accidental	unintentional
indifferent	apathetic	disinterested
isolate	detach	quarantine
jargon	argot	slang
jovial	genial	merry
judge	estimate	referee
justification	excuse	reason
juvenile	adolescent	immature
keen	clever	observant
label	brand	classify
labour	toil	work
lead	direct	proceed
lean	slim	thin
leave	abandon	desert
liberal	copious	unrestrained
liberal	lenient	open-minded

limitation	boundary	constraint
lucid	clear	understand
lucky	auspicious	fortunate
mad	furious	irate
manage	administer	control
manipulate	control	shape
marginal	borderline	limited
match	agree	correspond
maze	complexity	labyrinth
meditate	ponder	think
memorial	commemoration	monument
mention	allude	refer to
merge	blend	fuse
narrow	confined	restricted
nature	aspect	character
necessary	mandatory	requisite
negate	contradict	refute
negligent	careless	remiss
negotiate	bargain	deal
nice	affable	benign
noble	aristocratic	distinguished
novice	beginner	Non Profes
nuisance	annoyance	offense
obedient	faithful	loyal
objection	disapproval	protest
obligatory	compulsory	required

observe	notice	watch
obvious	conspicuous	definite
offend	anger	irritate
offer	bid	proposal
omen	premonition	sign
omit	exclude	remove
opportune	advantageous	auspicious
pacify	appease	placate
pain	ache	discomfort
paramount	chief	leading
partisan	biased	dogmatic
passive	inactive	lethargic
pause	break	cease
permeate	diffuse	disseminate
perpetuate	endure	preserve
perplex	astonish	baffle
persecute	afflict	harass
radiate	effuse	emanate
radical	basic	fundamental
range	anger	furore
rank	arrange	classify
realize	accomplish	fulfil
recalcitrant	obstinate	stubborn
receptacle	container	repository
reconcile	atone	conciliate
regret	deplore	grieve

reliable	dependable	trustworthy
sanction	approval	permit
scope	aim	extent
section	division	portion
settle	adjust	compromise
shallow	superficial	trivial
shrewd	careful	calculating
significant	distinctive	important
slight	delicate	slender
spontaneous	impromptu	unplanned
spread	announce	broadcast
stabilize	balance	steady
tame	domesticate	subdue
tangle	intertwine	twist
temper	mood	nature
tendency	inclination	trend
term	cycle	duration
thrift	conservation	prudence
tough	aggressive	unyielding
transfer	convey	exchange
tumult	agitation	commotion
turbulent	disordered	violent
vain	boastful	inflated
valid	authorized	legitimate
variety	assortment	diversify
verify	authenticate	substantiate

ANTONYMS

absence	presence
accept	refuse
accurate	inaccurate
advantage	disadvantage
alive	dead
always	never
ancient	modern
answer	question, query
approval	disapproval
approached	receded, departed
abundant	scarce
admit	deny
advance	retreat, retire
artificial	natural
arrival	departure
ascend	descend
attack	defense
attractive	repulsive
attention	inattention
asleep	awake
ally	enemy
agree	disagree
bad	good
backward	forward, onward
bend	straighten

beautiful	ugly
beginning	ending
below	above
bent	straight
big	small, little
blunt	sharp
better	worse
best	worst
blame	praise
bless	curse
bitter	sweet
borrow	lend
bravery	cowardice
build	destroy, demolish
bold	timid, meek
bright	dull
broad	narrow
clear	vague, cloudy
careful	rush, careless
calm	troubled
capable	incapable
captivity	freedom, liberty
cellar	attic
cheap	dear, expensive
close	distant
clever	stupid

cold	hot
combine	separate
clockwise	anti-clockwise
correct	incorrect
conceal	reveal
come	go
common	rare
comfort	discomfort
courage	cowardice
cruel	kind
courteous	discourteous, rude
cunning	simple
dainty	clumsy
danger	safety
dark	light
deep	shallow
decrease	increase
definite	indefinite
demand	supply
despair	hope
disappear	appear
disease	health
discourage	encourage
dismal	cheerful
doctor	patient
dry	wet

dull	clear, bright
dusk	dawn
early	late
easy	difficult
ebb	flow
East	West
economize	waste
encourage	discourage
entrance	exit
employer	employee
empty	full
excited	calm
end	beginning
expand	contract
expensive	inexpensive, cheap
export	import
exterior	interior
external	internal
fail	succeed
false	true
feeble	sturdy, strong, powerful
foolish	wise
fast	slow
few	many
famous	unknown
forelegs	hind legs

fat	thin
find	lose
first	last
freedom	captivity
fold	unfold
frequent	seldom
forget	remember
found	lost
fresh	stale
friend	enemy
fortunate	unfortunate
frank	secretive
full	empty
generous	mean
gentle	rough
gather	distribute
glad	sorry
gloomy	cheerful
giant	dwarf, pygmy
granted	refused
great	minute, small, little
guardian	ward
guest	host
guilty	innocent
happy	sad, miserable
hard	soft

harmful	harmless
hasten	dawdle
hate	love
healthy	unhealthy, ill
here	there
heavy	light
height	depth
hero	coward
hill	valley
horizontal	vertical
hinder	aid, help
honest	dishonest
humble	proud
hunger	thirst
imitation	genuine
immense	tiny, minute
imprison	free
include	exclude
increase	decrease
inhabited	uninhabited
inferior	superior
inside	outside
intelligent	unintelligent, stupid
inhale	exhale
interior	exterior, outside
interesting	uninteresting, dull

internal	external
intentional	accidental
join	separate
junior	senior
justice	injustice
king	subject
knowledge	ignorance
laugh	cry
lawful	unlawful
lazy	industrious, energetic
land	sea
landlord	tenant
large	little, small
last	first
lawyer	client
lecturer	student
lender	borrower
lengthen	shorten
left	right
less	more
light	dark, heavy
like	dislike, unlike
likely	unlikely
leader	follower
little	large, much, big
lofty	lowly

long	short
loud	soft
loss	find, win
low	high
loyal	disloyal
mad	sane
magnetize	demagnetize
master	servant
mature	immature
maximum	minimum
me	you
merry	mirthless, sad
minority	majority
miser	spendthrift
misunderstand	understand
narrow	wide
near	far, distant
neat	untidy
new	old
night	day
noisy	quiet
North	South
obedient	disobedient
odd	even
offer	refuse
open	shut

optimist	pessimist
out	in
parent	child
past	present
patient	impatient
peace	war
permanent	temporary
please	displease
plentiful	scarce
poetry	prose
possible	impossible
poverty	wealth
powerful	feeble, weak
polite	impolite, rude
private	public
prudent	imprudent
pretty	unsightly, ugly
pure	impure
qualified	unqualified
rapid	slow
regularly	irregularly
rich	poor
right	wrong, left
rigid	pliable, soft
rough	smooth
satisfactory	unsatisfactory

security	insecurity
scatter	collect
serious	trivial
second-hand	new
sense	nonsense
shopkeeper	customer
singular	plural
simple	complicated
slim	thick, stout
solid	liquid
sober	drunk
speaker	listener
sour	sweet
sorrow	joy
sow	reap
stand	lie
straight	crooked
strong	weak
success	failure
sunny	cloudy
take	give
tall	short
tame	wild
teacher	pupil
thick	thin
tight	slack, loose

top	bottom
transparent	opaque
truth	untruth, lie
up	down
vacant	occupied
valuable	valueless
victory	defeat
virtue	vice
visible	invisible
voluntary	compulsory
vowel	consonant
wax	wane
wisdom	folly
within	without

WORDS OFTEN CONFUSED

Words that sound alike or nearly alike but have different meanings often confuse us and cause writers trouble. Let us look at a few of the most common pairs.

Accede, exceed

Accede means to agree, to allow.

Exceed means to go beyond, to surpass.

Accept, except

Accept means to receive

He accepts defeat well.

Except means to take or leave out.

All the students, except Rajesh, went for the picnic

Affect, effect

Affect means to influence.

Lack of proper rest may affect the quality of your work.

Effect, n., result, v., to accomplish.

The effect of his speech was such that every organization wanted to work with him.

A lot, Alot

A lot (two words) means many.

The students have a lot of work to do; hence they may be late for lunch.

'A LOT' (one word)-Not the correct form

Adapt, adept, adopt

Adapt means to adjust.

Adept means skilled.

Adopt means to take as your own.

"Some people cannot adapt to new surroundings."

"He is very adept at dodging awkward questions."

"He tends to adopt the attitudes of those around him."

Addition, edition

Addition is something that is added.

Edition is a particular version, issue or publication of a book, play, etc.

Adverse, averse

Adverse means inauspicious, hostile.

Averse means disinclined, repelled.

'I'm very much averse to making a long, arduous journey under such adverse weather conditions.'

Advice, advise

Advice is the noun.

Advise the verb.

Affect, effect

Affect is a verb.

Effect is more usually a noun. When used as a verb it means to achieve, fulfill, realize.

Aloud, allowed

Aloud means out loud, speaking so that someone else can hear you.

Allowed means permitted.

Altar, alter

Altar is the table in a church.

Alter means to change.

Already, all ready

Already means by this time.

The food was already finished when I reached the mess.

All ready means prepared.

Dinner was all ready when the guests arrived.

All right, alright

All right is the correct form.

Alright is grammatically incorrect.

Allusion, illusion

Allusion is an indirect reference or hint.

The professor made an allusion to Shakespeare's work.

Illusion means deception or mirage.

They saw a mirage: that is a type of illusion one sees in the desert.

All ways, always

All ways means by every way or method; always means all the time, forever.

Amoral, immoral

Amoral describes someone who has no morals.

Immoral describes someone with low morals.

Annual, annul

Annual means yearly; annul means to make void or invalid.

Anyone, any one

Anyone means anybody, any person at all.

Any one means any one person and is followed by "of".

"Does anyone else want to come along with us?"

"Any one of you is welcome to come along with us."

Appraise, apprise

Appraise is to assess or estimate.

Apprise is to inform or notify.

He was asked by the management to appraise the situation and apprise them of the possible solution.

Ascent, assent

Ascent is an upward movement.

Assent means agreement.

Assistance, assistants

Assistance means help or aid.

'Assistants' is the plural of assistant, one who gives help.

Assure, ensure, insure

Assure means to guarantee.

Ensure means to make sure.

Insure means to protect against loss or damage:

Bazaar, bizarre

Bazaar is an exhibition or fair.

Bizarre means weird, grotesque, alien.

Berth, birth

Berth is a place to sleep on a boat or ship. Birth is the beginning (usually of life).

Beside, besides

Beside means by the side of.

Besides means in addition to.

Biannual, biennial

Biannual means happening twice a year; biennial means every two years.

Board, bored

Board is a long sheet of wood, also a group of people as in "Board of Directors", and as a verb means to go onto a ship, plane or other form of public transport.

Bored means not interested.

Born, borne

Born is always the beginning of life.

Borne means carried.

I was born in Delhi.

The logs were borne down the river to the mill.

Bought, brought

Bought is the past tense of buy.

Brought is the past tense of bring.

Brake, break

Brake means to stop.

Break means to smash.

Breath, breathe

Breath, noun, means air inhaled or exhaled.

You could see his breath in the cold air.

Breathe, verb, to inhale or exhale.

If you don't breathe, then you are dead.

By, buy, bye

By is a preposition meaning next to.

Buy means purchase.

Bye means farewell or good-bye.

Canvas, canvass

Canvas is cloth or fabric.

Canvass means to seek votes, to survey, to sell door-to-door.

Caught, court

Caught is the past tense of catch.

Court is a place where criminals are tried.

Cereal, serial

Cereal is something you might eat for breakfast, such as porridge.

Serial is something in a series; something that continues one after another.

Coarse, course, cause

Coarse means rough-textured or scratchy;

Course (apart from its use in "of course") is a noun meaning: route, track, a raceway; progression, development; plan, plan of action;

A Cause as a noun means origins, beginnings; grounds, justification; an ideal or belief; a case or lawsuit. As a verb it means lead to, result in, and make happen.

Collaborate, corroborate

Collaborate means to work with someone;

Corroborate means to establish the truth of something.

Compliment, complement

Compliment means praise or congratulate. You always pay someone a compliment, not a complement.

Complement means to supplement, round out.

Continual, continuous

Continual means something that happens frequently, with breaks between the occurrences.

Continuous means something that happens without stopping!

Continual interruptions distract me from my study.

The continuous noise of your television distracts me from study.

Conscience, conscious

Conscience means the sense of right and wrong.

The student's conscience kept him from cheating on the exam.

Conscious means to be awake

I was conscious when the burglar entered the house.

Co operation, corporation

Co-operation means working together;

Corporation is a business organization.

Copyright, copy write

Copyright is the legal ownership of a book, film, play, piece of artwork, musical composition, etc, or the right to print, publishes, film, record or performs them;

Copy write is something you do if you are creating advertising or publicity material.

Correspondence, correspondents

Correspondence is written communication;

Correspondents are those who write it.

Creak, creek

Creak is both a noun and a verb and means squeak or groan (for instance, rusty hinges and loose floorboards creak);

Creek is a noun and means a waterway or stream.

Credible, creditable

Credible means believable;

Creditable means praiseworthy or deserving credit.

Criteria, criterion

Criterion is singular;

'Criteria' is plural.

Currant, current

Currant is a fruit, usually dried.

Current as an adjective means contemporary, fashionable; as a noun it means stream, flow.

Desert, dessert

Desert means to abandon (and can also be a noun, meaning a wasteland);

Dessert is the sweet course of a meal.

Device, devise

Device is a noun, meaning a gadget or (particularly in writing terms) an invention;

Devise is a verb, meaning to invent or plot.

Elicit, illicit

Elicit means to extract or draw out;

Illicit means not legal.

Eminent, imminent

Eminent means distinguished, famous;

Imminent means near, close at hand.

Fair, fare

Fair means average, good-looking, pale, and unbiased.

Fare is the money you pay to go somewhere by bus, train, plane, taxi, etc. It can also refer to a passenger. As a verb it means do, as in:

He didn't fare as well in his exams this year.

Farther, further

Farther is used for physical distance;

Further for non-physical.

The farther we walked the more hostile the terrain became.

He promised to give the action plan further thought.

Flare, flair

Flare means to flash or blaze and (as a noun) is a pyrotechnic device;

Flair means ability or skill.

Foreword, forward

Foreword is the preface in a book, usually written by someone who is not the author.

Forward means ahead, near the front.

Forth, fourth

Forth means forward.

Fourth is after "third".

Foul, fowl

Foul can mean dishonorable (by foul means), disgusting (a foul smell), entangle (rubbish dumped in the river can foul fishing lines);

Fowl is a bird.

Found, founded

Found is the past tense of find;

Founded means started, as in "My great grandfather founded this company nearly a hundred years ago."

Hail, hale

Hail means to greet or to come from (as in, She hails from India) and as a noun it is frozen raindrops.

Hale means healthy or (as a verb) to haul.

Hanged, hung [Both are 'hang' in the Present Tense]

A criminal is always hanged.

A picture is hung.

We hung the portrait where everybody could see it.

John Smith was hanged yesterday at dawn.

Herd, heard

Herd is a group of animals.

Heard is the past tense of hear.

Here, hear

Here refers to a location (as in "over here").

Hear is always what your ears do.

Hole, whole

Hole is an opening.

Whole means complete.

Idle, idol

Idle means inactive, lazy.

Idol is something that is worshipped or (in the case of a person) looked up to as a hero.

Incite, insight

Incite is a verb that means to stir up; encourage: Talk like this is likely to incite a riot.

Insight is a noun meaning intuition; awareness; understanding.

Intolerable, intolerant

Intolerable means tiring, onerous crushing.

Intolerant means biased, prejudiced.

Knew, new

Knew is the past tense of know.

New is the opposite of old.

Later, latter

Later means afterwards.

Latter is the second of two things.

Lessen, lesson

Lessen means to make less.

Lesson is something you learn.

Lose, loose

Lose always means mislaying or dropping something and not being able to find it,

Loose means slack or free:

Manner, manor

Manner means method, appearance, class, character.

Manor is strictly a large, stately house.

Mantel, mantle

Mantel is the shelf above a fireplace, or the fireplace surrounding.

Mantle is a cloak or blanket.

No, know

Strange that these two should get confused, but they do.

No is always the opposite of yes.

Know is to be certain (that you know the difference!)

Overdo, overdue

Overdo means to exaggerate or carry something too far.

Overdue is what your bills are when you forget to pay them.

Passed, past

Passed is the past tense of pass.

Past means a time that has gone.

Peace, piece

Peace means the absence of war (or even noise)

Piece is a portion of something.

Plain, plane

Plain means obvious, also unadorned or lacking in good looks.

Plane is a carpenter's tool or an abbreviation of airplane.

Patience, patients

Patience means forbearance.

Patients are people under medical care.

Perspective, prospective

Perspective means point of view.

Prospective means future, inevitable, destined.

Pour, pore

You pour sauces, gravies, etc, over your dinner, while pore means to study something—so, "pore over the book", not "pour over the book", which reads as though you might be damaging the book with an unnamed liquid substance!

Practice, practise

In British usage, practice is always the noun and practise the verb.

Pray, prey

Pray is usually what you do when you talk to God.

Prey as a verb means to hunt, to stalk,; as a noun it means the subject of the hunt.**Principal, principle**

Principal means chief or main, also the amount borrowed in a loan.

Principle means regulations or ideals.

Quiet, quite

Quiet means without noise.

Quite when used in fiction usually means moderately, but can also mean totally or entirely.

Raise, raze

These two are exact opposites. Raise means to lift or build up and raze means to pull down

We will raise the reputation of our village to new heights.

He instructed his army to raze the village to the ground.

Reality, realty

Reality is real life.

Realty is real estate.

Reference, reverence

Reference is something referred to

Reverence means respect.

Residence, residents

Residence is a house.

Residents are the people who live there.

Respectfully, respectively

Respectfully means politely.

Respectively means in the order stated.

Sale, sail

Sale is either offering something for purchase ("for sale") or offering it at a special price ("on sale").

Sail is part of a ship or boat.

Scene, seen

Scene is the place where something happens.

Seen is the past participle of see.

Sever, severe

Sever means to separate, detach.

Severe means grim, stern.

Site, sight, cite

Site always refers to location or place: building site; archaeology site.

Sight always refers to vision, as in the clichй 'a sight for sore eyes'.

Cite means to summon, or to refer to a source.

Some time, sometime

This is a common confusion. Some time is a period of time and sometime means at some time not specified.

Some time ago you promised to take me out for lunch.

Sometime when you're not busy we must take the kids for a movie again.

Stationary, stationery

Stationary means standing still.

Stationery refers to writing paper.

Straight, strait

Straight means without bends.

Strait is a passage of water.

Tenant, tenet

Tenant is one who rents a property.

Tenet is a principle or belief.

There, their, they're

There is a location: "Put it over there."

Their is the possessive of they: "their coats"

They're is short for they are.

To, too, two

To is a preposition meaning towards; too means also or extremely (as in "You are speaking too fast for me"); two is the number after one.

Through, threw

Through is a preposition meaning in and out of.

We drove through the tunnel.

Threw is the past tense of throw.

Verses, versus

'Verses' is the plural of verse, something a poet writes.

Versus means against, or in comparison with something or someone.

Wary, weary

Wary means careful.

Weary means tired.

Wave, waive

Wave means to flap your hand in farewell and as a noun is also a breaker on the beach.

Waive means to give up one's rights or claim.

Weak, week

Weak is the opposite of strong.

Week is seven days, Sunday to Saturday.

Weather, whether

Weather has to do with meteorological conditions, climate.

Whether is a conjunction of condition (a bit like the word if)

Whether it rains or shines, I have to go.

Whose, who's

This confusion is similar to its and it's.

Whose is possessive, and who's is short for 'who is'.

Your, you're

Your is possessive and you're short for "you are".

ONE WORD SUBSTITUTION

1.	One who is out to subvert a government	Anarchist
2.	One who is recovering from illness	Convalescent
3.	One who is all powerful	Omnipotent
4.	One who is present everywhere	Omnipresent
5.	One who knows everything	Omniscient
6.	One who is easily deceived	Gullible
7.	One who does not make mistakes	Infallible
8.	One who can do anything for money	Mercenary

9. One who has no money	Pauper
10. One who changes sides	Turncoat
11. One who works for free	Volunteer
12. One who loves books	Bibliophile
13. One who can speak two languages	Bilingual
14. One who loves mankind	Philanthropist
15. One who hates mankind	Misanthrope
16. One who looks on the bright side of things	Optimist
17. One who looks on the dark side of things	Pessimist
18. One who doubts the existence of god	Agnostic
19. One who pretends to be what he is not	Hypocrite
20. One incapable of being tired	Indefatigable
21. One who helps others Good	Samaritan
22. One who copies from other writers	Plagiarist
23. One who hates women	Misogynist
24. One who knows many languages	Polyglot
25. One who is fond of sensuous pleasures	Epicure
26. One who thinks only of himself	Egoist
27. One who thinks only of welfare of women	Feminist
28. One who is indifferent to pleasure or pain	Stoic
29. One who is quite like a woman	Effeminate
30. One who has strange habits	Eccentric
31. One who speaks less	Reticent
32. One who goes on foot	Pedestrian
33. One who believes in fate	Fatalist
34. One who dies without a Will	Intestate

35. One who always thinks himself to be ill	Valetudinarian
36. A Government by the people	Democracy
37. A Government by a king or queen	Monarchy
38. A Government by the officials	Bureaucracy
39. A Government by the rich	Plutocracy
40. A Government by the few	Oligarchy
41. A Government by the Nobles	Aristocracy
42. A Government by one	Autocracy
43. Rule by the mob	Mobocracy
44. That through which light can pass	Transparent
45. That through which light cannot pass	Opaque
46. That through which light can partly pass	Translucent
47. A sentence whose meaning is unclear	Ambiguous
48. A place where orphans live	Orphanage
49. That which cannot be described	Indescribable
50. That which cannot be imitated	Inimitable
51. That which cannot be avoided	Inevitable
52. A position for which no salary is paid	Honorary
53. That which cannot be defended	Indefensible
54. Practice of having several wives	Polygamy
55. Practice of having several husbands	Polyandry
56. Practice of having one wife or husband	Monogamy
57. Practice of having two wives or husbands	Bigamy
58. That which is not likely to happen	Improbable
59. People living at the same time	Contemporaries
60. A book published after death of its author	Posthumous

61. A book written by an unknown author — Anonymous
62. A life history written by oneself — Autobiography
63. A life history written by somebody else — Biography
64. People who work together — Colleagues
65. One who eats too much — Glutton
66. That which cannot be satisfied — Insatiable
67. One who questions everything — Cynic
68. A flesh eating animal — Carnivorous
69. A grass eating animal — Herbivorous
70. One who lives in a foreign country — Immigrant
71. To transfer one's authority to another — Delegate
72. One who is a newcomer — Neophyte
73. That which is lawful — Legal
74. That which is against law — Illegal
75. One who is unmarried — Celibate
76. A game in which no one wins — Draw
77. A study of man — Anthropology
78. A study of races — Ethnology
79. A study of the body — Physiology
80. A study of animals — Zoology
81. A study of birds — Ornithology
82. A study of ancient things — Archaeology
83. A study of derivation of words — Etymology
84. Murder of a human being — Homicide
85. Murder of a father — Patricide
86. Murder of a mother — Matricide

87.	Murder of an brother	Fratricide
88.	Murder of an infant	Infanticide
89.	Murder of self	Suicide
90.	Murder of the king	Regicide
91.	To free somebody from all blame	Exonerate
92.	To write under a different name	Pseudonym
93.	A thing no longer in use	Obsolete
94.	A handwriting that cannot be read	Illegible
95.	Words written on the tomb of a person	Epitaph
96.	One who is greedy for money	Avaricious
97.	Something that cannot be imitated	Inimitable
98.	One who doesn't know how read and write	Illiterate
99.	A person's peculiar habit	Idiosyncrasy
100.	An animal who preys on other animals	Predator
101.	Violating the sanctity of a church	Sacrilege
102.	One who can throw his voice	Ventriloquist

Chapter 22

Reading Skills

Learning Objectives

- To know the importance of Comprehension
- To study the importance of Précis
- To understand the use of Paragraphs for Reading and Comprehending

Comprehension

Comprehension means the ability to understand a given text. It is therefore an exercise aimed at improving one's ability to read and to understand the direct, implied and the hidden meaning of the given text.

Comprehending a given passage helps to improve the ability to read in between the lines and also improves the expression of an individual and is considered an important tool to judge the level of understanding of an individual.

From the business point of view as well, comprehending a given text is very important, because many a times you are required to give a quick reading to various texts, business reports, etc and understand the important issues. Thus, even for managers being able to comprehend a text is of utmost importance.

Basically, you need to learn the tactics of comprehending a given text and be able to express in your words, the important points in the text and the theme of the text.

Your power of observation needs to be very good to be able to grasp the essential details.

Precis

A precis is a summary of a given text, however lengthy the text may be. The text may be report a speech or findings or record.

It is again a good exercise for improving your reading, analyzing and writing skills. But remember you should be able to comprehend first and then any you can summarize effectively.

All essential details should be included in the summary; as the purpose of precis writing is to convey the main idea of the text in a highly condensed or concise form.

Precis writing has its use in today's busy and competitive business world, where summary of lengthy documented is prepared, especially for the superiors those who do not have enough time to go through the entire text.

Although, there is no hard and fast rule regarding the length of the precis but the length should be approximately one-third the original length.

Precis writing is an art and a good communicator can have a high degree of perfection. There are certain areas where precis are much required and appreciated.

- To apprise the top management of the views of the committee members.
- To apprise the management of the government policy statements.
- To apprise the management of the taxation proposals and their implications.

All professionals such as, lawyers, journalists secretaries of executives need to excel the art of precis writing regularly.

Paragraphs for Reading and Comprehending

Given below are some paragraphs related to various topics.

Read and try to summarize each one of them.

Also analyze and discuss about each paragraph in groups.

Paragraph 1

<u>URBANIZATION V/s. INDUSTRIAL ZONES</u>

Unchecked urbanization in the midst of industrial zones, often at variance with the law, is an issue which has been the cause of litigation between the Municipal Corporation and chemical units in Thane for the last few years.

The controversy was in the spotlight again last month when residents of housing complexes surrounding the Bayer (India) factory at

Thane complained of ill health because of a leak of hazardous gas on 31 January.

The Bayer plant is among the six units operating in Thane which have been classified as hazardous. The other units are Colour Chem, Sandoz (Clariant), Indofil and Piramal Healthcare's two units (Roche and Boeringer Mannheim). These units have been involved in litigation since the 1980s over the construction of residential blocks in their vicinity-something that is forbidden by the law after the Bhopal disaster.

However, the Thane Municipal Corporation (TMC) and the builders have so far managed to brow-beat these units and at least three of the six units are contemplating moving out of Thane. The litigation between these units and the builders and the TMC reached its climax in September 1996, when the apex court instructed the Union environment department to constitute an authority to study the problem and give its report, which would be binding on the Maharashtra Government.

While the Supreme Court had initially suggested that the factories should shift out of Thane, better counsel apparently prevailed and the Court gave the expert committee, constituted in November, the power to decide on the issue.

But the committee report, which was to be completed within three months, is likely to be delayed.

Meanwhile, the residents of Raheja, Dadlani and Willows complexes have stated a campaign against the pollution problem they face from these units and especially from the Bayer plant, which though at least a kilometer away, is posing the most serious problem to them.

And, after the 31 January incident, the residents have enhanced their efforts to get' organized and make these companies more accountable in terms of providing information about the processes they employ inside the factory.

After the 31 January incident, the residents of these complexes petitioned the local municipal authorities, the local police and the state pollution control board. It is because of their efforts, they claim, that Bayer accepted that a gas leak had, indeed, occurred.

Paragraph 2

<u>**A World Class Company: Aby Accounting**</u>

For more than 80 years, Aby Accounting held a stellar reputation as an accounting firm of the highest integrity.

Yet in 2002, the firm was found guilty of obstruction of justice in the investigation of BSL Corporation. Subsequently, a whole list of its clients announced their accounts had to be redone because of irregularities.

For example, among these clients was telecommunications giant W B Com, which had to restate $9 billion in revenues, and whose chief financial officer was subsequently arrested for fraud. Clearly, Aby's organizational culture itself had undergone a transformation from ethical to unethical. But how did this occur?

In the early 1990s, Aby Accounting was a highly respected company with 85,000 employees worldwide. People were proud to be a part of the team, and their experience in the company helped them build their careers.

At that time, Aby had formal ethical standards and ethics training, although no ethics office. It even had a consulting group whose actual business was training other companies in ethics.

A key company motto originated by founder Aby John and cherished over the years was "Think straight talk straight." Company lore included the story of a young Aby pushing back on a railway executive who wanted him to cook the books. Andersen replied, "There's not enough money in the city of Chicago to induce me to change that report."

However, over the years the company's profits came increasingly form consulting rather than from auditing. According to newspapers, and an Aby employee beginning in 1995, the company's emphasis on ethics morphed into an emphasis on profits.

A mismatch of standards and approaches between the accounting side, and the consulting side of the company developed, but was never addressed. This failure to clearly define corporate values left such determinations to individuals and groups, who were encouraged to focus on the bottom line and retain customers by keeping them happy.

In addition, the firm's culture favored working with hot New Economy companies, high-risk clients who were doing massive acquisitions and who were talking advantage of government deregulation to transform themselves.

In this fast-paced environment, new and complicated ethical considerations were easily overlooked.

Furthermore, according to researchers, tradition became translated into unquestioning obedience to the partner, no matter what one was asked to do.

For example, managers and partners were expected to pad their prices. Reasonable estimates for consulting work were simply doubled or more as consultants were told to back into the numbers." New consultants were advised not to bother with corporate training because it interfered with lucrative client contacts.

In the end, it was the loss of its ethical culture that led to the downfall of Aby Accounting. Employees had adopted the attitude that people in the company are all good and ethical people, so ethics training and ethics manuals and ethical offices were all irrelevant.

If we put ourselves in their shoes at the time, we can imagine that was a legitimate view. But it could also have been a convenient rationalization.

Paragraph 3

<u>PERU: A COUNTRY ON THE MOVE</u>

Peru is a country on the move. A country where stability, sustained economic growth, reintegration into the financial community, political stability, and a peaceful atmosphere prove that dramatic changes have occurred.

At the beginning of the nineties, a new economic program was implemented in order to end the crisis in which the country found itself. Based on an economic stabilization plan, a program of structural reforms and measures in order to re-integrate Peru into the international financial community was established.

Peru began to reap the benefits of this program in 1993. Inflation fell to 49.5 percent for that year and continued to descend, reaching 10:2 percent in 1995. Between 1993 and 1995, the economy grew at an annual average of 8.6 percent, the highest growth rate in Latin America, and foreign reserves, which in 1990 had reached negative levels, today stand above US $8.5 billion.

In this way, over the last few years Peru has turned into one of the most open and dynamic economies in the region, and is without doubt a country with a very bright future.

Foreign investment in Peru, attracted by a stable, transparent and consistent legal framework, with clear rules and a high growth potential in various sectors of the economy, has now reached US $10.5 billion.

Peru, a country of contrasts and natural beauty, is preparing for tourism to turn into one of the key players of the economy. The Machu Picchu citadel, the Sacsayhuaman fortress and the Ollantaytambo archaeological center in Cuzco, the tombs of the Lord of Sipan and Sican in Lambayeque, the Quelap fortress in Amazonas, the ChanChan city of clay in La Libertad and the Chulpas de Sillustani in Puno are only some of the magnificent archaeological sites found all around the country.

But Peru also has nature, offering magnificent natural parks and ecological reserves, from the deepest tropical rain forests to the most breath – taking sites in the heights of the Peruvian Andes. The diversity of this country of contrasts – its folk-lore, handicrafts and delicious food – makes it one of the most outstanding places to visit on the planet.

Agriculture is another sector with enormous growth potential, given the extraordinary natural characteristics which allow it to produce a great variety of high quality products all year round. Products such as camu-camu (already available in the Japanese market as a soft drink with a high vitamin C content), asparagus, broccoli, artichokes, high quality coffee, a wide range of tropical fruits and cochineal, source of a natural dye widely used in diverse industries, are only a few examples of high quality Peruvian exports.

Mining, fisheries, infrastructure and the manufacturing sectors also offer attractive investment opportunities.

However, the great challenge for Peru today is to turn its economic achievements into improvements in the quality of life for all Peruvians and to continue to reduce poverty.

Economic success cannot be an objective in itself, but an instrument to achieve the objective and that greater objective is our goal.

Paragraph 4

The Year of the Eve

The Scottish ewe Dolly has forced advanced biological research to the top of the agenda of every ambitious nation)

While humankind has enjoyed the fruits of physics, chemistry and informatics in this century, the quality of life in the next world will be enhanced by development in biology and informatics. That is why there is a scramble among nations to acquire key technologies in these two areas.

Scottish embryologist Ian Wilmut and his colleagues at Roslin Institute at Edinburgh have come in from behind and demonstrated the possibility of cloning large mammals like sheep, using the master copy of a cell m an adult sheep and have earned kudos from the scientific world.

They have also activated the tabloid press and uninformed rabble rousers to raise the possibility of the Hollywood film Boys from Brazil-where an obsessed Nazi scientist raises dozens of clones of Adolf Hitler in a secret laboratory in Brazil-turning fiction into fact. When the dust settles down, Dolly will enter history as a landmark in human understanding of life and its-reproduction.

Leaving aside the questions of desirability or otherwise of cloning being applied to human beings (the debate would • be endless), what is most impressive is the technological advance in experimental biology in a very short time of about a quarter century.

To take a single microscopic cell, remove the tinier nucleus containing the genetic information from it; similarly remove the nucleus from an egg which contains only half the genetic information and replace it with what had been removed from the earlier cell, subsequently reactivating adult genes before being ensconced in the womb of a surrogate mother for foetal development and later birth, is a scientific achievement of the highest order.

The fact that a not-so-large company had funded this research shows that many forward -looking companies think that focused biological research will have economic benefits for patrons and it also demonstrates that one does not have to be in the laboratories of a multi-billion dollar drug company to be doing cutting edge work in biology. It is to be noted that even in the US, which is far ahead in both biotechnology and informatics, most innovative work has been done in small companies and laboratories.

Though there are at least half a dozen active and competent research groups working in genetic engineering and molecular biology in India, there have been no spectacular results despite the creation of a separate Department of Biotechnology in the Central Government.

There may be scores of reasons for this state of affairs. However, with a reasonable abundance of scientific talent in India and jobs in biotechnology being quite wall paying in recent years, hopefully Dolly will inspire more bright young Indians to study biology (and not computer science alone) and come up with idea-based research that is intellectually satisfying and commercially exploitable.

Paragraph 5

DIABETES AND BLINDNESS:

Diabetes is a familiar disease. Go to any party or family gathering, you may come across one or two persons not taking sweets because they are diabetic.

It is common knowledge now that diabetes is a disease caused by deficiency of a hormone called insulin and the patient may have to take anti-diabetic drugs or insulin injections.

Unfortunately, however, for most of the general population this is as far their knowledge of diabetes goes.

In fact, only a minority of diabetic patients are aware of the possible implications of this chronic disorder.

Diabetes mellitus is in fact a multi-system disease and in addition to delayed wound healing and inflections it may cause neuropathy, nephropathy, retinopathy and a host of the other problems.

Diabetic retinopathy is already a leading cause of treatable blindness in the Western world and is fast becoming a major cause of blindness in India also.

In addition to retinopathy, diabetics also have an early onset of senile cataract which again leads to visual impairment.

What is diabetic retinopathy?

Retina is the neurosensory thin film in the eye which perceives visual signals from outside and sends them to the brain. If retina is diseased vision will definitely be affected.

Diabetes affects the minute blood containing capillaries supplying the retina and they either become occluded or start leaking. The result is edema, exudation and hemorrhages on the retina. If the macula which is the most sensitive part of the retina is affected it leads to severe impairment of vision. Occlusion of retinal capillaries produces a lack of oxygen supply to the retina which responds by production of new vessels.

These new vessels bleed frequently, causing large hemorrhages in front of the retina and blocking vision. In late stages of the disease even detachment of the retina may occur and blindness may result.

How to tackle this problem?

Unfortunately, in its early stages diabetic retinopathy may produce no symptoms and by the time a patient develops visual impairment and contacts an eye surgeon, some irreparable damage may have already occurred. It is for this reason that periodic eye check up of all diabetic patients is strongly recommended.

Diabetic retinopathy is usually a late complication of diabetes and usually occurs approx., a decade after the onset of diabetes.

Food control of diabetes helps in delaying the onset of this disease.

Laser photocoagulation: Laser photocoagulation has made the treatment of diabetic retinopathy possible and is now easily available in India. Science has harnessed the power of laser beams and used the transparent medium of eye to treat various eye diseases including this.

For diabetics it is advised to remember the following points:

- Good metabolic control of diabetes.
- Periodic eye checkup with eye specialist, at least every 6 months.

Paragraph 6

<u>**MAKE LIBRARIES READER - FRIENDLY**</u>

(Niti Paul Mehta on the apathy in most schools towards libraries that leave this resource unexploited to the extent it deserves)

A library is often described as a repository of knowledge. Students call it the 'reference centre'. It contributes in diverse ways to the entire educational process. A library is essentially an extended limb of a school and plays both a complementary and supplementary role in the overall educational effort of a school.

At present there is a general apathy in most schools towards this institution and the resources inherent in it are not being exploited to the extent they deserve. There is an imperative need to motivate students to not only visit the library 'regularly but also to make use of the facilities available to them in a meaningful manner. Teachers and the librarian can guide students bỹ recommending' what books or reading material can benefit them most.

Reading can serve as a medium for-healthy, meaningful diversion, But most students go to the library with a more serious purpose. They go there to get some information or to get some material on some subject or to consult some reference book to authenticate what they, already know or to get some book issued in their name, Most students visit the school library to supplement or expand on the knowledge they have already gained in the classroom. Occasionally, a student might go to the library to sit in its quiet environment to learn his lesson.

But one basic, the most important role of the library, is to inculcate, feed and nurture a reading habit in students at the school stage. Another important and related aspect is to guide the students to grow into discerning readers. They should become capable of deciding for themselves what to read and what to avoid and what to digest and retain out of what they read.

The reading habit once formed becomes a life – long possession which continues to inspire and add new dimensions to one's personality all through one's life. Unfortunately, due to the onslaught of TV and the video boom, the home environment has become uncongenial to those interested in reading. The reading habit is fast becoming a casualty. In the context of satellite invasion, the role of the school library gains even greater significance.

Once more unfortunate aspect is that libraries, especially in the Capital's government schools are ill-organized, neglected and ill-equipped to function efficiently.

In most Delhi schools the library is housed in a room having the same dimensions as an average classroom. The total space available is often just enough for keeping the almirahs containing books.

It looks more like a 'store' than a library. To be functionally useful, even a modest school library ought to newspapers/magazine stands, long tables along both sides of which some 60 to 70 students can be accommodated at one time.

At present lack of sufficient space is one main reason which has rendered many a school library non-functional. In such a situation even the best of librarians feels handicapped.

Another limiting factor is the officially approved pool of books out of which alone schools can purchase books. As a result the choice becomes restricted. This list of approved books is revised from time to time but it is done in a very cursory and superficial manner. For the most part the list remains the same. There is a need to make the exercise of revision of this list more meaningful. A library is a progressive institution and to be of real worth it must be kept updated.

A library has a distinct character. The environment inside it is different from that of a classroom. It is noise-free. In a perfect scenario of quietude students sit and read or study without any distraction. In fact, entering the sombre atmosphere of the library ought to be an educative experience in itself.

One imbibes such useful values as self-discipline, respect for the other person's need, good etiquettes, polite speech, courtesy, the ability to share, the capacity to think and analyze things independently besides a host of other technical values which one acquires from the study of certain specific subjects.

In a library a student is in the company of like-minded fellow students. Even otherwise he is in good company. He is in the company of books. To have a good, well-equipped school library is a fundamental right of a student.

Paragraph 7

<u>SMOKING AWAY YOUR HEALTH</u>

(Views of a Doctor on smoking)

First and foremost let us go around the world and update our knowledge of the news in recent weeks regarding smoking and its effects.

Scientists have warned in a new global survey that deaths from cigarettes are likely to more than triple over the next quarter century to 20 every minute around the world.

According to a researcher at the Imperial Cancer Research Fund, "In most countries the worst is yet to come. If current smoking patterns persist then by the time the young smokers of today reach middle or old age there will be about ten million deaths a year from tobacco, one death every three seconds, he added.

Another recent news item states that four out of five woman smokers are addicted to nicotine, making it difficult for them to quit the habit. The American Centre for Disease Control and Prevention said that after a survey of nearly 8,000 woman smokers, it was found that 81.2% reported at least one indicator of nicotine addition, such as feeling dependent on cigarettes, needing more cigarettes to get the same effect, feeling unable to cut back on smoking or feeling sick when they do.

According to the director of CDC, one of the major reasons people fail to quite smoking is the difficult dealing with withdrawal symptoms. CDC said that 73% female smokers want to quit but find it, difficult to do so.

Even among women who smoked less than six cigarettes a day, over half reported a symptom of nicotine addition. CDC also estimates that 61,000 women aged 35 or higher died from smoking related cardiovascular diseases in 1990.

As far as women are concerned, I was always under the impression that since less number of Indian omen were given to smoking there was definitely no fear for Indian women from smoking yet lately I've been hearing about more and more women smokers and surprisingly from the RURAL than URBAN areas and from UNEDUCATED more than the EDUCATED.

One of my very sincere patients comes from a village in Haryana an works in a government office in Gurgaon. He had continuous cough for a month or so. When he was cured he asked me if he could bring his mother, "of course", I said "why not?" He said his mother also suffered from chronic cough and he wanted me to cure her.

I did not understand his hitch in bringing her to me. Initially he said he would try to bring her, I thought may be she felt sick while travelling as he is a daily commuter by train so the difficulty was in bringing her.

It came as quite a surprise, when he came the next time and when I questioned him about bringing her, very meekly he replied that she refused to come as she knew that the first thing I would do was to stop her BIDI SMOKING which she COULD NOT AND WOULD NOT irrespective of the cough.

Another aspect about women smokers in India is that since there has been a trend toward equality with men young girls in colleges and universities do not hesitate to smoke openly along with men.

Little do they realize that this quality may lead them to equality in susceptibility to tobacco-induced diseases and may be death? They fail to realize that their children may be malformed, remember men still do not get pregnant, and future would be bleak for coming generations.

Have you noticed a chain smoker's condition in the mornings? He is unable to use his hands in the presence of others and shies away from meting people in the morning, e.g. if he has to go and meet the bank manager or put his signatures on some paper or even write anything he would prefer to do so unobserved as he fears that people will notice the trembling of his hands.

This tremor prevents him from having even a cup of tea or a glass of water when offered in front of outsiders.

The reasons being that the very act of picking up the tea cup may spill the tea or even keeping the cup back may be difficult due to these tremors.

In this context, it would be proper for me to write about the primary and the secondary actions of any drug be it alcohol, tobacco, opium, coffee or even antidepressant tablets that are used indiscriminately these days.

If the primary action of any drug is to pacify your body and mind, the secondary action which is bound to follow would be to cause restlessness, or sleepless or even depression. So the best way is to indulge as less as possible or avoid any drug in any form.

To further elaborate, in my article on alcohol where, I've described the three stages of man in a drinking session, the first two stages those of the fox and the wolf are primary actions of alcohol and the secondary action that is completely diverse is that of his behavior like a swine (pig). He, who makes plans to conquer the world in the first two stages, is unable to even attempt his daily functions in the last stage.

Of course in homoeopathy we have 'remedies' for all these problems. We do not call them 'medicines' but remedies as they have remedial action on the ills of the body and not medicinal action to suppress those ills. The remedies can be Nux vomica, Pulsatilla, Caladium, Staphysagria, Digitalis, Glesemium or even Tabacum. Here I must warn all readers, though I often write the names of the remedies, not to do any self-medication, please see a doctor, as the susceptibility of the patient and appropriate potency for individual patients can be determined only by a homoeopath.

Test Yourself

1. What is the importance of Comprehension?
2. Explain the importance of Précis.

Chapter 23

Common Errors

Learning Objectives

- To study the commonly occuring errors in Grammar
- To understand the errors by going through the incorrect & correct versions of a sentence

COMMON ERRORS

INCORRECT	CORRECT
I love with my friend.	**I love my friend.**
He resembles with his father.	**He resembles his father.**
She jumped in the pool.	**She jumped into the pool.**
What is the time in your watch?	**What is the time by your watch?**
Our examinations begin from Monday.	**Our examinations begin on Monday.**
He does not agree to you.	**He does not agree with you.**
You have eaten nothing from yesterday.	**You have eaten nothing since yesterday.**
I invited all my friends for tea.	**I invited all my friends to tea.**
Govind works hardly.	**Govind works hard.**
I came directly from Agra.	**I came direct from Agra.**
This story is much interesting.	**This story is very interesting.**
The boy is not a student of our college whom you met near the gate.	**The boy whom you met near the gate is not a student of our college.**
This is an unique proposal.	**This is a unique proposal.**
He did not wanted to go for the party.	**He did not want to go for the party.**
Either of you have to do this work by Monday.	**Either of you has to do this work by Monday.**
Mathematics are my favorite subject.	**Mathematics is my favorite subject.**
None of the two boys could give the correct answer.	**Neither of the two boys could give the correct answer.**
This is a better scheme.	**This is a good scheme.**
This is a good scheme than the one you suggested yesterday.	**This is a better scheme than the one you suggested yesterday.**
This is best scheme that you ever suggested.	**This is the best scheme that you ever suggested.**

Our college stands nearest to the Metro station.	**Our college stands next to the Metro station.**
There are any apples in the fridge.	**There are some apples in the fridge.**
There aren't some apples in the fridge.	**There aren't any apples in the fridge.**
The doctors have given up little hope they had.	**The doctors have given up the little hope they had.**
I am very obliged to you for your help.	**I am much obliged to you for your help.**
Unless he does not work hard, he will not pass the examination.	**Unless he works hard, he will not pass the examination.**
Why are you angry upon me?	**Why are you angry with me?**
He has gone to abroad for higher studies.	**He has gone abroad for higher studies.**
He signed with red ink.	**He signed in red ink.**
The Indian cricket team succeeded to win the match.	**The Indian cricket team succeeded in winning the match.**
There is no harm to try your luck.	**There is no harm in trying your luck.**
He does not listen the advice of his superiors.	**He does not listen to the advice of his superiors.**
Have you ordered for stationery as yet?	**Have you ordered stationery as yet?**
You should not violate against the rules of the country.	**You should not violate the rules of the country.**
Please send the books on my address.	**Please send the books to my address.**
I have eat my food.	**I have eaten my food.**
He has send me the books.	**He has sent me the books.**
My small niece is learning alphabets these days.	**My small niece is learning alphabet these days.**
He has bought two dozens of oranges.	**He has bought two dozen oranges.**

The plane, with all its crew, were hijacked.	**The plane, with all its crew, was hijacked.**
He is good in English.	**He is good at English.**
I have no pen nor pencil.	**I have no pen or pencil.**
He congratulated me for my success.	**He congratulated me on my success.**
He will return just now.	**He will return presently.**
Can you open this knot please?	**Can you untie this knot please?**
Who is it? It is me.	**Who is it? It is I.**
Vijay has been ill since two days.	**Vijay has been ill for two days.**
He obtained just passing marks.	**He obtained just pass marks.**
I worked as fast as I can.	**I worked as fast as I could.**
Always tell the truth .	**Always speak the truth.**
His English knowledge is poor.	**His knowledge of English is poor**
It is a good house to live.	**It is a good house to live in.**
Girls of this college are very good.	**The girls of this college are very good.**
He is our immediate neighbor.	**He is our next door neighbor**
Please borrow me some money	**Please lend me some money.**
This book deals in common English errors.	**This book deals with common errors**
His brother deals with sugar.	**His brother deals in sugar.**
He is leaving his service.	**He is leaving his job.**
Fair out of these notes.	**Make a fair copy of these notes.**
I felt pity on the beggar.	**I took pity on the beggar.**
Go now and enjoy.	**Go now and enjoy yourself.**
All his relations are poor.	**All his relatives are poor.**
He behaves as if he is the king.	**He behaves as if he was the king.**
The joker did nothing but laughed.	**The joker did nothing but laugh.**